REFLEXIVE EMBODIMENT IN CONTEMPORARY SOCIETY

SOCIOLOGY *and* SOCIAL CHANGE

Series Editors: *Alan* **Warde,** *Nick* **Crossley, University of Manchester**

Published titles

REFLEXIVE EMBODIMENT IN CONTEMPORARY SOCIETY

Nick **Crossley**

Open University Press

Open University Press
McGraw-Hill Education
McGraw-Hill House
Shoppenhangers Road
Maidenhead
Berkshire
England
SL6 2QL

email: enquiries@openup.co.uk
world wide web: www.openup.co.uk

and Two Penn Plaza, New York, NY 10121-2289, USA

A catalogue record of this book is available from the British Library

ISBN 0 335 21697 8 (pb) 0 335 21698 6 (hb)
ISBN 13 9780 335216 970 (pb) 9780 335216 987 (hb)

Typeset by BookEns Ltd, Royston, Hertfordshire
Printed in Poland by OZ Graf S.A.
www.polskabook.p.

This is for Michele and little Jakey (18 months).
The two brightest stars in a happy sky.

Contents

Series editor's preface

In response to perceived major transformations, social theorists have offered forceful, appealing, but contrasting accounts of the predicament of contemporary western societies and the implications for social life and personal well-being. The speculative and general theses proposed by social theorists must be subjected to evaluation in the light of the best available evidence if they are to serve as guides to understanding and modifying social arrangements. The focus of the series is the critical appraisal of general, substantive theories through examination of their applicability to different institutional areas of contemporary societies. Each book introduces key current debates and surveys of existing sociological argument and research about institutional complexes in advanced societies.

Nick Crossley's book ranges across core areas of contemporary social sciences – social theory, the body and health, popular and consumer culture, and social and personal identity. Part One outlines several major contributions to the social theory of the body and embodiment. It develops a lucid critique. Part Two reviews diverse empirical studies relevant to evaluating theoretical claims. The organizing themes are highly topical – obesity, objectification, body maintenance and body presentation activities. This varied material is supplemented by the author's own original research, which sustains a distinctive and coherent account of how zones of bodily practice come to be inhabited unequally by different social groups. A contribution in its own right to the theory of the body, this book is original and challenging and will be of interest not only to students but also, because of its vibrant argument, as a stimulus to reflection and debate among specialist scholars.

Alan Warde

Acknowledgements

This book was written during research time granted to me jointly by the Sociology discipline area and the Centre for Research in Socio-Cultural Change (CRESC) at the University of Manchester. Thank you to both for making this extended period of leave possible.

Intellectually, the book has been influenced by the many third-year undergraduates who have taken my 'Body and Society' course at Manchester over the six or seven years that it has been running. The course is a vehicle which has allowed me to shift my thoughts on embodiment from questions of dualism to questions of reflexivity and to begin to get my head around some of the embodied practices that shape our bodies in contemporary society. The demands, comments, criticisms, recommendations and encouragement that students have offered in that process of transition have been invaluable.

I would also like to thank Alan Warde, who suggested that I write this book and offered support along the way, and Simon Williams, whose ideas and projects have played their usual role of kick-starting me into action.

At 18 months my son Jake has been too busy to offer much intellectual input and has no doubt had to bite his tongue when he has spotted flaws in the argument. He has done more than his fair share of the emotional work, however, and has a wonderful knack for taking my mind off writing when this is necessary. Finally, thanks as ever to Michele. Her contributions are too numerous to mention but juggling her own busy schedule to let me get this written has certainly been a big one.

Introduction

This book is about reflexive embodiment in contemporary Western societies. In the present chapter I will map out the way in which I will tackle this issue. Before I do, however, I need to unpack my subject area. I begin with a discussion of what I mean by reflexive embodiment.

What is reflexive embodiment?

'Reflexive embodiment' refers to the capacity and tendency to perceive, emote about, reflect and act upon one's own body; to practices of body modification and maintenance; and to 'body image'. Reflexivity entails that the object and subject of a perception, thought, feeling, desire or action are the same. When I look in the mirror, for example, I am both the subject who sees somebody in the mirror and the object who is seen. Likewise, when I wash I am both the object who is washed and the subject or agent who does the washing. There is no necessity to this coincidence of subject and object. When I was a baby my mum washed me, much as I now wash my son. And when I look in my driving mirror I see other people behind me. But when the object and subject are the same we have reflexivity.

In defining our relations and actions towards our bodies as reflexive I am making an assumption; namely, that we are our bodies. If I were something other than my body then my relation to my body would not be reflexive because the subject and object in the relationship would be distinct beings. In the context of the history of philosophy this notion that we are our bodies is a contestable assumption. The founder of modern philosophy, René Descartes, writing at the dawn of the modern era, famously argued both that mind and body are two distinct substances and that his real essence lay in his mind (Descartes 1969; Crossley 2001). Furthermore, in making this claim he was drawing, in part, on religious ideas which are still adhered to by some today – ideas of an immortal soul which separates from the body upon death. From this point of view my body and I are two different things, even though I am embodied in the sense that I reside, as a soul, within a body. In common with most contemporary philosophers and social scientists, I do not accept this dualist position. I have explained some of my reasons for this elsewhere (Crossley 2001) and will not reiterate them. Suffice it to say that I am persuaded that we are bodies, nothing more and nothing less, and thus that our relations to and actions upon 'our bodies' are reflexive.

Having said that I reject dualism, it is important to concede that reflexivity generates a lived sense of separation (or perhaps of separation and connection) between self and body. As I explain in Chapter 7, it entails that we turn back upon ourselves, generating a temporal split between subject and object and, as the terms suggest, objectifying ourselves. Our embodiment is experienced, to an extent, in a manner akin to an external object, such that we might be led to deem it, incorrectly, as external to our true self. This is reflected in our references to 'the body'. Talk of 'the body' objectifies our embodiment but at the same time abstracts and separates it from our being as a whole. It creates a sense of dualism and risks the category error that some philosophers have identified as the foundation of dualist thought (Ryle 1949; Crossley 2001). At the same time, however, this object that is abstracted from us in reflexive consciousness is also experienced as a possession and thereby reintegrated into our self and identity. We talk about 'my body', what 'I' am going to do to 'it', what 'it' looks like. 'I' and 'it' are clearly distinguished but 'it' is identified as 'my' possession: for example, 'Does *my* bum look big in this?', 'I wish I didn't *have* curly hair', 'I'm going to get *my* nose done.' Building upon Gabriel Marcel's (1965) formulation, therefore, we must conceive of our embodiment in terms of the twin aspects of 'being' and 'having'. Human bodies exist in two dimensions. We are our bodies (being) but sometimes perceive them as an object that we possess (having) and which we might experience, in some contexts, as taken from us (alienated) by way of the actions of others: for example, when they exercise authority over our body or when we become uncomfortably aware that they are staring at us and using our image for their own purposes, without our consent (see also Turner 1984; Bartky 1990).

The body can be objectified and 'constructed' in many ways, acquiring various representational meanings which both shape and are shaped by different practices of modification and maintenance. Compare, for example, those religious groups who regard the body as sinful and seek to mortify it by way of self-flagellation, with contemporary 'health cults' who valorize the body as the source of life and attribute to it needs which their members seek to service. We must be attentive to this variability of meaning and must be sure to understand reflexive bodily practices in accordance with the meanings of their practitioners. I do not mean to suggest that meaning, as a property of perception or discourse, comes before or independently of practice. The body can take on a meaning for us as a consequence of the way in which we learn to use it. Engaging in exercise, for example, may change my perception of my body and the meaning it has for me. Meaning and practice each shape the other in a continuous interaction. My point is simply that we must be attentive to meaning as well as practice. One of my criticisms of much contemporary 'grand theory' surrounding reflexive embodiment will be that it fails to penetrate the meanings actually attached to practice by social agents at the concrete and lived level.

Bodies are not simply passive objects that we manipulate and project meanings on to, however. Our bodies can resist the meanings we attempt to impose upon them, as when illness reveals a vulnerability I was not previously aware of and falsifies my claim to be 'fine', or grey hairs and aches and pains call my youthful self-image into question. Bodies change in ways that we have not anticipated, sometimes as unintended consequences of our actions, sometimes because they (we) are biological and physical beings, shaped by forces, elements and relations beyond the social domain, at least in the pure definition of that domain usually employed by sociologists. Bodies get fatter, lose fitness and, if left unattended, become smelly and unkempt. They do not stay the same if we choose not to maintain them and our maintenance work must accommodate their dispositions and tendencies. Moreover, to reiterate, bodies are subjects and agents in the reflexive process. It is central to the concept of reflexive embodiment that body modification and maintenance are embodied practices. 'Body work' is physical labour that we, qua bodies, perform upon ourselves. In some cases this may involve more than one person, an interaction and perhaps a division of labour. Although individuals can tattoo or pierce themselves, for example, it is more common to be tattooed or pierced at a parlour by an expert. The agent does not literally modify his or her own body in these cases but the practice is still reflexive inasmuch as, by the fact of contemplating a change to 'my body', he or she has occupied the twin roles of subject and object, and because modification involves embodied skills and work, albeit on behalf of another agent. My body modifies your body through the mediation of physical tools and techniques. In many cases, moreover, the individual him- or herself performs whatever body work is required. We clean our own teeth, wash ourselves, shave ourselves, brush our own hair, jog ourselves fit, etc.

Collective bodies

So far I have framed reflexivity in individual terms. There are important collective aspects that we must be attentive to, however. First, 'society', 'social groups' or 'populations', as embodied phenomena, can be and often are the object of reflexive discourse and intervention. The discourses and interventions associated with public health are an obvious example. Their focus is not the body of the individual but the collective body. Likewise, the subject of such reflections is not the individual but, at the very least, an individual representative of the social body and more often a network of representatives, teams, committees, etc. Even at the individual level, however, reflexive embodiment is achieved by way of the mediation of practices which are, in some degree, diffused within and derived from a collective – practices which the individual has not invented for herself, which may both pre-date and outlive her, and whose 'rules', 'logic' or 'feel' she has had to learn. Practices can become so deeply engrained within the pre-reflective, habitual life of our bodies that we either cease to notice that we perform them or experience them as 'natural instincts' or 'common sense'. As such they seem individual. Without denying the existence of either individual habits or biologically rooted dispositions, sociology liberates us, where appropriate, from these 'attribution errors', demonstrating that much of what seems personal and natural, because it has become a part of us, derives from the social world. My approach is sociological in precisely this sense. I am interested in reflexive embodiment as a collectively rooted aspect of individual life – that is, in terms of practices.

This is not to say that I have no interest in the individual practitioner. I do. Indeed, as will become apparent, individuals, their experiences, decisions and relative autonomy all play an important part in my schema. However, to add another key concept to that of practices, I believe that individual human agents fully become who and what they are through immersion in social practices and social relations. The isolated individual is a myth. This is not to the detriment of individuality and autonomy. Rather, it is a prerequisite of both. We become 'individual', in any meaningful sense of the term, and we become 'autonomous', as a consequence of the transformative experience, which begins at the moment of birth, of involvement in social relations and practices. This presupposes that we are 'something' at birth; that we are born with both generic capacities/potential and individually variable dispositions. We are not blank slates. But what we are by birth is a far cry from the autonomous individual celebrated in contemporary Western societies, and in so far as we ever approximate that ideal we do so by virtue of our involvement in collective life.

Body and society

In recognizing this social, collective dimension, we must be careful to avoid two erroneous implications. First, we must be careful to avoid drawing the implication that reflexive embodiment is merely a mechanism by which 'society' controls and moulds the body, and not only because of the problematic assumptions such claims make in respect of 'society'. Against this I will argue, to reiterate, that socially rooted reflexivity forms a basis for human autonomy and choice. Though social interactions, relations and groups are a source of rules, norms and mechanisms of control, they equally constitute a context wherein we develop the capacity to make decisions and act upon them, including decisions which deviate from social norms and resist social pressures. In addition, I am keen to emphasize that both social and personal control of the body are necessarily limited in their reach and effects by virtue of: the relative autonomy of biological processes and structures; the unintended impact of social and individual behavioural changes upon the body; and the multiple blind spots within our reflexive relations to our body, at both individual and collective levels. These limits to reflexivity are a key theme in later chapters of the book.

Second, we must avoid the implication that because society affects the body it is somehow not 'of' the body; that it is disembodied. Societies emerge out of and depend for their continued existence upon the embodied interactions of social agents. Practices are done, roles are played or performed and processes are effected by the embodied work of agents. No aspect of the social world exists independently of such embodied activity. However, this does not mean that we can reduce society down to the level of individual bodies or biological structures. Just as consciousness emerges, as an irreducible structure, out of the biochemical interactions and relations which comprise the human organism, and out of the interaction between that organism and its immediate environment, so too interaction between conscious human agents generates emergent social phenomena, such as norms, body techniques (see Chapter 8), roles, networks, power relations, social systems, social positions and institutions which are, by definition, irreducible to the particular individuals who embody them at any particular point in time, and which pre-date, 'constrain' and will outlive them. The social is nested in the psychological, which is nested in the biological, which is nested in the chemical and so on, but at each level we find irreducible phenomena. Durkheim recognized this many years ago:

> even if society is a specific reality it is not an empire within an empire; it is part of nature and, indeed, its highest representation. The social realm is a natural realm which differs from the others [e.g. the chemical, biological and psychological realms] only by a greater complexity.
>
> (Durkheim 1965a: 31)

This does not preclude conflict between emergent levels, nor does it imply that society can be studied in the same way as other structures of the natural world. The relative autonomy of social structures necessitates that they are studied by distinct methods and can lead to the generation of demands which are in conflict with lower-level biological or psychological inclinations and demands. For example, social groups may seek to control biopsychologically rooted dispositions and tendencies which are disruptive to their image of a good or civilized life, as Freud (1986), Elias (1994) and Durkheim (1965a) himself argued. In this respect, furthermore, the chain of influence connecting different levels of the natural world is not merely upwards, from biology and psychology to the social world, but also downwards. Society impacts back upon the biological and psychological structures that sustain it. Indeed, the very notion of a hierarchy of levels is redundant. Biological, psychological and social structures are each interacting and sometimes conflicting structures within a wider whole. Interaction is not the same as 'merging', however. Indeed, it makes sense to speak of interaction only in so far as these levels retain some relative autonomy. We need to be mindful of both interaction and relative autonomy in our account.

The society in question

I have said that this book is about reflexive embodiment in contemporary Western societies. This is not because reflexive embodiment is in any way specific to such societies. Indeed, most accounts of contemporary forms of body modification draw comparisons with those of earlier times and/or non-Western cultures, indicating that reflexive embodiment was/is different but nevertheless present in such societies. I will touch upon some of these comparisons, at least tacitly, as I must if I am to make claims about contemporary Western societies.

My focus is upon contemporary Western societies rather than the contrast between them and other societal types, however.

Having said this, there are two senses of 'contemporary' in the book, deriving from the different focus of the writers I have consulted. And in the process of writing the book I have been struck by the comparisons and contrasts that seem to keep emerging between them. Some of the literature on reflexive embodiment is focused upon the pattern of social life that began to take shape in the eighteenth century, a pattern of social life that is often classified as 'modern' and 'industrial'. Other writers focus on the period from the 1970s onwards, a period that has variously been termed 'post-industrial', 'postmodern' and 'late modern', to name but a few. I do not have the space to rejoin the debates that have surrounded these terms and their various referents. I will deal with the issues raised when and where they arise, as and if they are relevant. It is important to be mindful of these two senses of 'contemporary' in what follows, however, particularly in Part One of this book. At least some of the disagreements I identify between sociological perspectives and some of my own criticisms hinge upon claims regarding social change in the 1960s and 1970s. This does not completely undermine the claims of those who operate with a broader (and older) sense of 'contemporary' as there clearly are many respects in which society in the post–1970s era manifests the key features of the modern societies that began to take shape in the eighteenth century. There are both continuities and shifts.

The aims of the book

The literature on reflexive embodiment is large and growing. There is a healthy body of empirical material addressing a range of reflexive bodily practices, from tattooing and piercing, through clothing, to working out, jogging, bodybuilding, beauty treatments and cosmetic surgery (Featherstone 1982, 2000; Sanders 1988; Rosenblatt 1997; Pitts 1998, 2003; Monaghan 1999, 2001a; Sasatelli 1999a, 1999b; Sweetman 1999; Turner 1999; DeMello 2000; Entwistle 2000; Gurney 2000; Crossley 2004a, 2004b 2006). In addition, and one step removed from this, there are a number of 'grand theories' which were perhaps never intended as theories of 'reflexive embodiment' but which have become standard reference points in debates regarding it. The theories I have in mind are those of Giddens (1991), Elias (1994), Bourdieu (1984), Foucault (1979, 1980) and a number of feminist writers who are influenced, in many cases, by Foucault, among them Bartky (1990) and Bordo (1993).

This literature is exciting and interesting but problematic. Specifically, we lack the 'big picture' as far as reflexive embodiment is concerned. One would not expect the big picture from the empirical studies, focused as they are upon specific practices. They focus on details, as they should. However, this begs the question of how their diverse findings fit together. To my mind they describe 'regions' of practice which need pulling together in a broader map of the terrain. One of my key aims in this book is to begin the work of constructing such a map.

The existing 'grand theories' are useful in this respect but none is adequate.

In part this is because many of them were not intended as theories of 'reflexive embodiment' and come at the topic tangentially. In part it is because they and their representatives have not been particularly responsive to recent empirical work or were formulated before much work had been done. However, it is also because these theories are partial in both senses of the word. They seek to depict society as a whole in a very particular way: for example, as detraditionalized, civilized, class divided, disciplinary or patriarchal. And their contribution to the field is to offer a framework, such as 'the civilizing process' or 'the carceral network', which empirical researchers are invited to slot their work into. We are invited to look at 'this' practice as an example of 'that' theoretical contention or social process. This can be a valuable exercise, and certainly each of these frameworks has something to offer us, but that is the problem: each has something to offer but, as with the empirical contributions, we lack a means of pulling these contributions together. We need a meta-perspective. Or rather, we need to consider whether a meta-perspective is possible. This too, is an aim of the book: to move beyond the partial and tangential theories of reflexive embodiment towards a more comprehensive position.

I am not advocating eclecticism. I do not believe that we should mix a bit of Foucault with a bit of Giddens and add Bourdieu to taste. Rather, I am suggesting that we take a good look at what each perspective has to say about reflexive embodiment, at a basic level, bracketing out differences that we do not need to attend to, in an effort to see whether and how their claims might be compatible. To return to my earlier metaphor, and not for the last time, I want to construct a map which arranges the various 'regions' of practice they identify relative to one another to form a representation of the broader territory.

However, I only want to include ideas that stand up. I do not want to incorporate every idea, theory or observation that has ever been made about reflexive embodiment. Some will be wrong and all will have limitations. Another of my key aims, therefore, is to review the grand theories in terms of both their internal coherence and their empirical credibility.

My final aim is to offer my own reflections upon the relations, processes and practices involved in body maintenance and modification. In spite of all the research and all the theory, it seems to me that 'reflexive embodiment' is still something of a 'black box' that we theorize and research around without ever fully penetrating. We never pin down exactly what is involved. This is something I hope to address through a discussion of bodily absence (Chapter 6), reflexive body techniques (Chapter 8) and George Herbert Mead's (1967) fascinating account of the nature of selfhood and reflexivity (Chapter 7). Related to this, moreover, I want to highlight the blind spots in our reflexivity, to consider how bodily (biological) processes interact with social processes in non-reflexive ways, and to consider how reflexive bodily projects might be triggered or affected by unintended bodily changes which shock us or take us by surprise (Chapter 5). That is, I want to elucidate reflexive embodiment by, amongst other things, identifying certain of its limits and obstacles.

Plan of Part One

The book comes in two parts. In Part One I critically review the grand theories of reflexive embodiment referred to above. In Part Two I offer my own more positive contribution. The chapter plan for Part Two is given in a separate introduction to that part. The chapter plan for Part One is as follows. Chapter 1 reviews the respective theories of Durkheim and Giddens. Chapter 2 deals with Elias and Bourdieu. Chapter 3 deals with Foucault. Chapter 4 deals with theories of consumer society and with a number of feminist critics who have both contributed to the consumer society debate and, in some cases, added a feminist slant to Foucault's ideas. My outlines are schematic and in each case I consider some of the most pertinent criticisms of the perspective in question. A more general review of the theories as a whole is given in the Introduction to Part Two, in preparation for the work which follows in that half of the book.

Part **One**
Reviewing *the* **Field**

1 Identity, individualism *and* risk

As I explained in the Introduction, this first part of the book offers a systematic and critical review of the main perspectives on reflexive embodiment in contemporary sociology. In this first chapter I examine two positions: those of Durkheim and Giddens respectively.

Body modification in 'elementary' societies

Durkheim discusses body modification in *Elementary Forms of the Religious Life*, in the context of an analysis of aboriginal totemic clans. Members of these clans, he notes, often bear a symbol of their totem on their body. In some cases this is temporary and serves very specific ritual purposes. Often, however, clan members undergo permanent modifications. They tattoo or scar their body; they pierce; they stretch their neck, earlobes or lips; sometimes they knock out a tooth:

> They do not put their coat-of-arms merely upon things which they possess, but they put it upon their person; they imprint it upon their flesh; it becomes part of them, ... it is more frequently upon the body itself that the totemic mark is stamped; for this is a way of representation within the capacity of even the least advanced societies. It has sometimes been asked whether the common rite of knocking out a young man's two front teeth at the age of puberty does not have the object of reproducing the form of totem ...

> (Durkheim 1965a: 137)

Totems and totemic symbols, Durkheim believes, represent the clan itself as a collective. By physically bearing the mark of the totem or a related sign, he maintains, the individual identifies herself with her collective, thereby revivifying its identity and cohesion. By bearing the mark of the group the individual reinforces awareness of its existence amongst both insiders and outsiders and declares their allegiance to it. She reproduces the mechanistic form of solidarity characteristic of such elementary collectives and analysed at length by Durkheim (1964) in *The Division of Labour*. The practices emerge, he claims, because collectively the group generates both an *esprit de corps* that induces a desire within the individual to express their belonging and an external (to the individual) pressure to demonstrate loyalty. The body is the focus of these pressures and practices because it is the way in which we exist for others. The body sets the individual apart both physically and as a site of sensual experience. I am identifiable as an individual by virtue of my discrete bodily boundaries and existence, and my experience of the world is uniquely my own because it is localized within this discrete organic entity and reflects the unique position in the world that I inhabit at any moment in time. My body connects me to others at a primordial level, however, because it both makes me perceptible to them, positioning me within their field of experience, and affords me a sensual apprehension of their embodied being. At the basis of the social world is an intercorporeal intertwining of sensuous-sensible, because embodied, beings (Merleau-Ponty 1964, 1968a). Altering the body therefore has profound social significance. It affects our relations with others:

> tattooing should be the most direct and expressive means by which the communion of minds can be affirmed. The best way of proving to oneself and to others that one is a member of a certain group is to place a distinctive mark on the body.
>
> (Durkheim 1965a: 265)

This is just one way in which the group celebrates and consolidates its existence. The *esprit de corps* of the group is maintained by way of regular festivals and rituals, as well as collective stories and symbols, such as the totem. And these overlap with body modifications in so far as the latter signify, in various ways, the stories and symbols of the tribe, and are themselves performed as rituals at festivals. The modification of the body of an individual is usually an event for the whole community or at least a select group, as is proper to a ritual which marks the belonging of the individual to the group. Others bear witness to the marking of the individual and confer meaning upon it.

In addition to symbolizing basic group membership, Durkheim continues, body markings indicate social positions and distinctions within the group. In addition to the distinction between insiders and outsiders, there is often a distinction between men and women, and between children and adults. In relation to sex, natural markers, invested with meaning in culture, are rejoined by a variety of further alterations of the body which signify many different things, including beliefs regarding sexual difference, beauty and fertility. In the case of children and adults, transition from one status to the other is often marked, in sexually differentiated ways, by a rite of passage. Moreover, this very often involves some form of physical test, which can be painful. Often the body is cut or scarred. Durkheim suggests that such pain is integral to solidarity building. To fully make sense of his understanding of this, we need to be mindful of his contention that religions, and through them societies, are founded on a distinction between the sacred and the profane which, to put it crudely, maps onto a distinction between a group and its 'others' (e.g. outsiders and the natural world). Pain rituals, Durkheim suggests, symbolize a transcending of the profane and an accession to the sacred. Individuals achieve sacred status (i.e. full group membership) by overcoming the limitations of the flesh:

> we cannot detach ourselves from [the profane] without doing violence to our nature and without painfully wounding our instincts. In other words, the negative cult cannot develop without causing suffering. Pain is one of its necessary conditions.

(Durkheim 1965a: 351)

Enduring pain, he goes on to argue, is a way in which the individual is trained to put the interests of society above her own. Avoiding pain is one of the most natural of our reactions and consenting to endure it is therefore a clear indication of our willingness to defy our nature in favour of social duties and demands. In order for societies to survive, individuals must be prepared to subordinate certain of their own egoistic wishes and wants for the good of the group, and the group therefore demands of them that they both learn and prove that they are prepared to do this. Pain rituals play a crucial role in this respect.

This relates to a more general point about asceticism. All societies, Durkheim argues, place restrictions upon bodily activity and this is necessary:

> society itself is possible only at this price. . . . it is constantly doing violence to our natural appetites, just because it raises us above ourselves. If we are going to fulfill our duties towards it, then we must be prepared to do violence to our instincts sometimes and to ascend the decline of nature when it is necessary.

(Durkheim 1965a: 356)

In some cases these restrictions may serve the practical function of preventing behaviours which are disruptive to social order. Groups have to restrict outbursts of aggression, for example, otherwise they might collapse into Hobbes's (1971) war of each against all. In other cases, however, the function of asceticism is symbolic. As with pain rituals, individuals are expected to rise above their appetites in order to prove their loyalty to the group. The Muslim practice of Ramadan and the Christian practice of Lent may both be interpreted in this light. They are both tests of a devotion which, in Durkheim's view, is devotion to one's group.

This account suggests that collective life, which is a 'state of nature' for human beings, nevertheless generates demands which conflict with certain of our basic individual impulses. Belonging to a society demands that we compromise and that we learn to overcome and control these impulses. In the first instance this is a conflict between the particularism of the individual and the universalism of the group, and it is played out in overt social interactions, as when a parent reprimands a child for contravening a norm. As individuals internalize the demands of the group, however, it becomes an 'internal' conflict between conscience and impulse. Durkheim argues that it is the experience of this internal conflict which leads us to believe, incorrectly in his view, in the existence of an immaterial soul separate from the body. Talk of a 'soul', he argues, is a pre-scientific way of making sense of the moral pressure we sometimes experience within ourselves, a pressure which is internal and yet experienced as dissociated from our basic desires and derivative of a higher source. We are right to think that this pressure comes from a higher source than our individual body, Durkheim argues, but not because it descends from a spiritual realm. Its source is the inter-world of social interaction and the imprint it leaves upon our individual conscience.

The cult of the individual

The collectivism that Durkheim identifies in 'elementary' societies has been displaced in modern societies, he argues, by a 'cult of the individual'. We no longer celebrate the collective but rather the individual, or at least the individual is now the totem of the group and individualism a key value. The primacy of collective identity has given way to that of individual identity. In particular, many of the key philosophies as well as the law of modern, enlightened societies afford the individual a moral and existential privilege that was not apparent in earlier times. This theme of individualism in modern societies is central throughout Durkheim's work and there are points, even in his early studies, where it is explored via the body. In *The Division of Labour*, for example, he notes that the legal systems of Ancient Greek city-states often included prescriptions regarding dress, hair and beards. By Roman times, he continues, this aspect of law, though still evident, was less so. And in modern societies it has all but disappeared (Durkheim 1964: 159). Decisions about appearance are now made by the individual herself, albeit within accepted bounds. Likewise, he notes that customs linking forms of dress to particular occupations and classes, which in the Middle Ages were reinforced by laws prohibiting the lower classes from wearing certain types of clothing, have gradually disappeared. In modern societies, he notes, we are free to wear what we want. In addition, he notes how modern societies are characterized by increased geographical mobility and the formation of cities, wherein members of different national and regional cultures mix and meet. This generates an interplay of cultures, he argues, which tends to undermine the authority of specific cultures and unsettle traditions. The latter lose their taken-for-granted feel and grip as agents learn about different perspectives and lifestyles, giving way to individual choice.

It is necessary at this juncture to note a distinction in Durkheim's work between egoism and individualism, and to reflect briefly upon the 'body project' with which he is most famously associated: suicide. Individualism, for Durkheim, is a social phenomenon in a strong sense. It entails that the individual, as a moral category, is clearly articulated in law, morality and other cultural forms, such that the rights and duties of individuals are clearly proscribed and each individual recognizes and respects both self and other as individuals. Durkheim has a 'sociologized' version of Kant's (1948, 1997) moral theory. Individuals live as individuals but within a strong (individualistic) moral framework which derives from their social world. The individual is not set apart from society but very much a product of it. The moral idea and ideal of the individual belongs to the collective representations of society. It is a social ideal. And sentiments of the individual qua individual are products of collective experience. Furthermore, the modern individual, with all the noble faculties granted them by Kant, no less than the member of the aboriginal clan, rises above their animal nature to the extent that their society demands and trains them to. A 'man is a man only because he is civilised', Durkheim (1965a) argues, and civilization is an effect of collective interaction between individuals. The interaction of individuals and groups has, over historical time, given rise to a society and culture which, when internalized, make contemporary individuals what they are, allowing them to reproduce (and over time modify) that self-same society:

> the individual gets from society the best part of himself, all that gives him a distinct character and a special place among other beings, his intellectual and moral culture. If we should withdraw from men their language, sciences, arts and moral beliefs, they would drop to the rank of animals. . . . But on the other hand, society exists and lives only in and through individuals.
>
> (Durkheim 1965a: 388–9)

Egoism, by contrast, suggests a situation in which the binding power of society and culture has weakened, throwing individuals back upon their primary, animal nature. Selfishness and a lack of respect for others, the less civilized and thus less social aspect of the human condition, thrive in this context but so, too, does existential crisis because human meaning and identity, which derive from the collective, are amongst the casualties.

It is for this reason that Durkheim (1952) writes in *Suicide* of an 'egoistic' form of the act. The individual thrown back upon himself, less integrated in society, is more likely to become personally, psychologically disintegrated and is therefore more likely to harm himself, even to the point of self-destruction. Egoistic suicide is rejoined, moreover, by an anomic form, generated, as the name suggests, by the erosion of norms in societies undergoing change. As norms are eroded, Durkheim argues, the mind becomes less regulated and, in particular, expectations fall out of alignment with actualities, leading to disillusionment, depression and possibly self-harm. This is relevant to us since 'self-harming' behaviours, particularly those forms which fall short of suicide, belong within the remit of reflexive embodiment and have been identified as a growing problem in modern societies (NHS Centre for Reviews and Dissemination 1998). It has been argued, persuasively to my mind, that such behaviours are not, as psychiatrists sometimes assume, failed suicide attempts (Strong 2000; Cresswell 2005a, 2005b). On the contrary, they are means that individuals have for coping with deeply distressing experiences which, where successful, calm suicidal impulses, thereby allowing the individual to go on living (Strong 2000; Cresswell 2005a, 2005b). However, the connection with suicide and thus with Durkheim remains. The causes are the same even if self-harming short-circuits the suicidal trajectory. And Durkheim's analysis of egoism and anomie might therefore elucidate certain more worrying aspects of the trend towards reflexive embodiment in contemporary societies.

In some respects the argument about egoism and anomie is the other side of the argument in *Elementary Forms* (1965a), which might be read as suggesting that individuals are often prepared to harm themselves when they are strongly integrated in a group which demands this of them. Indeed, Durkheim (1952) makes just that argument in his study of suicide, with respect to its 'altruistic' form. High levels of group integration can override basic human impulses towards self-preservation in much the same way as low levels can, he claims. Modern-day suicide bombers perhaps exemplify this. Durkheim's main interest in this respect is in suicide but the argument potentially applies to other forms of body modification, particularly those which can be perceived to cause the individual pain or to threaten health and well-being.

Having said all this, to return to the thread of my earlier argument, Durkheim also offers us a framework for understanding reflexive embodiment in its modern, individualistic but non-egoistic, non-anomic forms. To reiterate, he points us towards a 'cult of the individual' which members of modern societies orient to and are expected to demonstrate loyalty to by way of their body work. The body is as important to demonstrations and celebrations of individuality as it is to demonstrations and celebrations of the collective. In addition to expressing group loyalty and belonging by way of our bodies, we can also express individuality.

Durkheim assessed

Atkinson's (2004) work illustrates this latter point. He interviewed 92 tattoo enthusiasts in an effort to explore their motivations for becoming tattooed and the meanings that their tattoos had for them. A majority said they did it because they wanted to 'be individual'. Atkinson draws upon the work of Elias (see Chapter 2) to make sense of this, but his argument resonates equally well with Durkheim's argument about the cult of the individual. Even if having a tattoo is not particularly unique, some people do it because they want to be an individual and, as Atkinson puts it, want to demonstrate their adherence to this key modern social value. Like the aboriginal male who allows his front teeth to be knocked out in order to demonstrate his loyalty to the clan, the tattooed individual seeks to prove their individuality to a social group which expects this of them.

Very similar results are reported in Gill *et al.*'s (2005) work, in which 140 young British males from a variety of social backgrounds were interviewed and asked about their body maintenance/modification practices. The overwhelming finding was that young men of all social backgrounds place great emphasis upon being individual and 'different'. What counted as individual differed between interviewees, though not in accordance with sociological variables such as class. Some wore designer clothes to express their individuality, for example, whilst others refused to wear designer clothes for this same reason. Practices and choices were uniformly framed in terms of individuality, however. Moreover, many other studies of reflexive bodily practices report a strong emphasis in accounts upon either individuality or selfhood (e.g. Davis 1995; Sweetman 1999; Black 2004). There is good evidence for a 'cult of the individual' in relation to reflexive embodiment.

There are problems with Durkheim's account, however. First, Elias (2001) disputes the linear assumption of Durkheim's thesis, suggesting rather that societies fluctuate between collective and individualistic phases. The experience of the world wars in the mid-twentieth century is a recent example of a collective phase. It is often claimed that wars generate collective sentiment. If this is so, but Durkheim is still right regarding the role of body modification in the generation of solidarity, we would expect war to register in reflexive bodily practices. There is some evidence for this. In a brief history of tattooing, for example, DeMello (2000) notes that the world wars stimulated a growth in patriotic and family-focused tattoos among the working class. Individuals expressed their loyalty to their primary groups by way of a mark on the body. And the nature of their marks further symbolized this loyalty. Tattoos involved national flags and symbols. They involved a lover's name or the now much derided 'Mum and Dad'. This finding supports Durkheim's contention regarding the link between body marking and social solidarity but transposes it into the present and also supports Elias's reservations regarding individualization as a linear trend.

Second, following on, however individualized society may be at particular times, collective forms, such as subcultures and social move-ments, are always evident and these modern 'cults' generally demand expressions of loyalty to their collective ideal which impinge on reflexive embodiment. Fan cultures, such as we find in relation to both football and pop groups, constitute one example of this; fans wear scarves and hats declaring allegiance and in some cases have club or group emblems tattooed on their bodies. Another example is the politics of dress and appearance that we find in some contemporary social movements and religions, not to mention the various forms of asceticism these collectives demand. There were many debates in the 1970s, for example, about how a feminist ought to dress and what 'pleasures' she ought to be prepared to forgo (Walter 1990; Scott 2005). In some part these were aspects of political strategy, but it would be naïve to deny that an aspect of collective identity building was involved (Melucci 1986). These collectives are interesting counter-examples to the cult of the individual. However, as I noted in respect of war tattoos, they suggest that the mechanisms of solidarity building that Durkheim pointed to, including those centred upon the body, have survived into modernity. Durkheim is right about the purpose of body modification but wrong about the demise of its collective-focused form.

Third, it is reasonable to speculate that anomie and widespread egoism generate a demand for contexts of belonging and integration in contempor-ary societies which subcultures and movements meet. This complicates our picture as it suggests that an individual who is affected by anomie or egoism may engage in extreme body modifications either because of this lack of integration or because it motivates them to join a tightly integrated subculture which demands modifications as a sign of loyalty. The same national society can produce both anomic/egoistic and altruistic body modifications. With this said, we can turn to Giddens.

Detraditionalization, self-narratives and risk

Giddens understands reflexive embodiment as an aspect of a broader process of the reflexive reconstruction of the self. Practices of body modification and maintenance are found in all societies, traditional and modern, he claims, but their meaning varies and has been transformed in modernity. Echoing Durkheim, he argues that practices of modification and maintenance in traditional societies tend to be embedded in collective rituals and serve a definite role or function – for example, as rites of passage. Again like Durkheim, however, he believes that modernization has dissolved many of these traditions. The practices of modification have acquired a new role in this context. Detraditionalization has removed traditional sources of status, identity and biographical trajectory, he argues. The questions of who we are as individuals and what we should do with our lives are no longer answered for us by cultural scripts and structural restraints. We are increasingly forced to answer these questions for ourselves; to reflexively construct a sense of our identity, biography and future trajectory. Our embodiment is central here both because it is the very substance of who we are and must necessarily be moulded to fit our identity choices, and because, as Durkheim noted, it is our principle means of announcing our identity to both ourselves and other people. Our external appearance is 'a means of symbolic display, a way of giving external form to narratives of self-identity' (Giddens 1991: 62). Reflexive embodiment is therefore part of a wider reflexive reconfiguration of the self in late modern societies:

> The body has always been adorned, cosseted and, sometimes, in the pursuit of higher ideals, mutilated or starved. What explains, however, our distinctive concerns with bodily appearance and control today, which differs in certain obvious ways from those more traditional preoccupations? ... The body becomes a focus of administrative power, to be sure. But, more than this, it becomes a visible carrier of self-identity and is increasingly integrated into life-style decisions which an individual makes.
>
> (Giddens 1992: 31)

> The body cannot be anymore merely accepted, fed and adorned according to traditional ritual; it becomes a core part of the reflexive project of self-identity. A continuing concern with bodily development in relation to a risk culture is thus an intrinsic part of modern social behaviour.
>
> (Giddens 1991: 178)

As the first of the two quotations above makes clear, self-identity is not the only modern social force shaping the body, according to Giddens. He makes reference to administrative power, too. I will return to that point in later chapters. For the moment it must suffice to note that this is little more than an aside for Giddens and that his key argument concerning reflexive embodiment centres upon its place within the broader narrative construction of the late modern self. This argument is advanced, moreover, by reference to the way in which the body has become, both in opinion and fact, more malleable in late modern societies. From behaviour modification through cosmetic surgery to sex realignment, the process of modernisation has involved a proliferation of means of transforming the body, removing what were previously fixed and stable attributes. The body has become 'a phenomenon of choices and options' (Giddens 1991: 8). Even if individuals have no desire to change their body in the more radical ways facilitated by modern technologies, the influx of new possibilities forces them to make a decision to stay as they are. The sense of necessity that once attached to particular practices and ways of life has been lifted and individuals have no choice, therefore, but to choose.

There are both similarities and differences with Durkheim in this account. Both writers emphasize individualism and the collapse of tradition. Where Durkheim identifies detraditionalization as a source of anomie, egoism and self-destructiveness, however, Giddens tends to see it as a liberation and opportunity. The positive side, for Durkheim, by contrast, resides in the emergence of a new, shared culture centred upon the individual: a collectively shared individualism. Moreover, in consequence, for him, the celebration of individuality is, in some respects, a celebration of society because the individual is the totem of modern society.

Detraditionalization and the new possibilities for bodily transformation are not the only factors shaping reflexive embodiment in late modern societies for Giddens, however. In addition, he notes the importance of risk (see also Beck 1992). Modern medicine, in particular, identifies numerous sources of risk to our health stemming from what we eat, how we behave and from pollutants in our external environment. Even hospitals are identified as sources of danger in the era of 'superbugs'. These risks shape our self-narratives and body projects. We become risk managers in relation to our embodied selves:

> All individuals establish a portfolio of risk assessment, which may be more or less clearly articulated, well informed and 'open'; or alternatively may be largely inertial. Thinking in terms of risk becomes more or less inevitable and most people will be conscious also of the risks of refusing to think in this way, even if they may choose to avoid those risks.
>
> (Giddens 1991: 126)

This is complicated, however, because, first, the discourse of risk deals in probabilities which are often difficult to put in perspective, especially for a lay public who lack statistical competence; second, some risks pull in contradictory directions, such that protecting oneself against one danger may increase one's vulnerability to another; third, the scientific advice is not always consistent, especially where different and competing camps of experts are involved, and even where it is, it sometimes changes over a relatively short time-span. The individual is forced to make difficult decisions in unclear circumstances. The way forward is not clearly prescribed and she must therefore take her own, existential step. She must choose for herself and, in doing so, choose herself.

Giddens concedes that at least some of us are inclined to ignore advice about risks in our environment, endeavouring to conduct our lives as we always have. In relation to this latter point, however, he reiterates the above point that we are, so to speak, condemned to choose. We do not have to change our eating habits in response to scientific advice about the dangers of certain foodstuffs, for example, or to give up smoking, but it is very difficult to avoid any awareness of that advice and thus we must actively choose to ignore it. We cannot live in ignorance of such risks as our ancestors did. We cannot behave in a 'traditional' manner because traditional action entails ignorance of the alternatives and absence of choice, but in our society we are bombarded with information and alternatives, and we are forced to choose. To give an example, Giddens argues that we are all 'on a diet'. What he means by this is not that we are all attempting to lose weight or all adhering to a particular regime, such as the Atkins diet or macrobiotics. Some of us may live on deep-fried Mars bars and chips. However, we still make a choice to reject the advice of health and beauty experts and we live with an awareness of alternatives. In that respect, our eating patterns are much less shaped by deeply engrained habits of tradition than they were in the past, and much more by reflection and decision.

Moral issues impinge here. The growth of vegetarianism, for example, whilst partly fuelled by health concerns, is often more directly related to concerns for animal welfare and the environment. And again these ethical concerns are sufficiently diffuse in the population for most adults to be aware of them. Meat eaters know that they eat meat when others choose not to. As such they cannot but regard their own meat eating as a matter of choice. Giddens theorizes this in terms of what he calls the 'life politics' of late modernity. Linking into arguments on so-called 'new social movements' (e.g. Melucci 1986), he suggests that the political configuration of late modern societies has changed. The traditional politics of emancipation, contested by left- and right-wing parties and movements, has been rejoined, if not eclipsed, by the emergence of a range of social movements which have raised a wide range of new moral issues – movements who have politicized and, to a degree, reshaped the practices of everyday life. All practices are embodied and, in this respect, the impact of the new social movements is of great significance in relation to reflexive embodiment. In some cases, however, this is even more so as the body is thematized in the discourse of new social movements. In addition to vegetarianism, for example, life politics embraces such issues as abortion, health, sexuality, the use of drugs, legitimate uses of the body and the alleged repression of possibilities for sensuality in the modern context. Body projects intersect with body politics.

Some critics have interpreted the trends Giddens describes, independently of him, in terms of a growing 'culture of narcissism' (Lasch 1984, 1991). This interpretation implies that agents are withdrawing from the world because they experience it as increasingly hostile and beyond their own control (Lasch 1984, 1991). They work upon the body because it is theirs and because it is in their control in a way which even other aspects of themselves (e.g. their job and marital status) are not. Giddens rejects these interpretations, adopting a more Durkheimian view of the body as a sign-bearer in social interaction. 'Body planning', he argues, is 'more often an engagement with the outside world than a defensive withdrawal from it' (Giddens 1991: 178). As such it is not narcissistic in the psychoanalytic sense intended by these critics. Agents modify and maintain their bodies with a view to projecting themselves outwards towards other people. However, he accepts that, in psychiatric terms, the so-called 'narcissistic disorders' and such 'pathologies of reflexive self-control' as anorexia nervosa have replaced others in the list of most likely disturbances in modern societies. Moreover, he notes a gender skew in this domain. Females, he observes, are much more vulnerable to eating disorders, including both anorexia nervosa and compulsive eating. This, he argues, is explained by the lack of opportunities and power afforded to women in contemporary society. Women turn to food and seek to control their eating in an effort to carve out a domain where they are in control. Where this becomes excessive it can spiral out of the woman's control and become a disorder. This is still related to the wider context of reflexive embodiment for Giddens, however. Taking back control could be accomplished in many ways. The reason why eating disorders in particular predominate is that they are extensions of the body regimes and reflexive self-control that characterize the lives of all agents within late modern societies.

Giddens assessed

Notwithstanding the differences between them, the same studies that support Durkheim's 'cult of the individual' tend to support Giddens too, even where the authors claim theoretical differences with him (e.g. Davis 1995). At the level of individual meaning, as noted above, qualitative research suggests that individuals understand their reflexive bodily practices as matters of choice which express individuality, selfhood and individual identity (e.g. Sweetman 1999; Atkinson 2004; Black 2004; Gill *et al.* 2005). Moreover, at least some of this work points to the significance of risk, inasmuch as agents either understand specific modifications (e.g. piercing) as risky and elect to manage that risk (see Sweetman 1999), or else engage in specific practices as a means of managing wider environmental and lifestyle-related risks. By the same token, however, the various objections and counter-examples to the individualization trend that we noted in relation to Durkheim stand in relation to Giddens. And there are further problems.

   McNay (1999) has argued that certain dispositions, specifically relating to gender, are so deep-rooted and engrained that we are both unlikely to spot them reflexively and unlikely to be able to change them if we do. She uses Bourdieu's conception of the habitus to capture this sense of deep-seated and pre-reflexive dispositions (see Chapter 2). Similarly, Calnan and Williams (1991) have argued that individuals do not routinely reflect upon themselves in the way Giddens suggests, at least with respect to matters of health, a fact which they argue is distorted by interview-based research which effectively generates the reflexive discourse it analyses by asking probing questions. Using a non-directive approach to interviewing, they note that agents do not spontaneously offer the kinds of reflexive accounts of health and the body that perspectives such as that of Giddens lead us to expect. Moreover, following this on and drawing from the thesis of the 'absent body' (see Chapter 6), Williams (1996) has argued that reflection of the kind described by Giddens is episodic, rather than chronic, and tends to be prompted by crises such as the onset of health problems. We think about our bodies when they go wrong but not otherwise. This also suggests that some groups in society may be more inclined to reflection, since their bodies are more conspicuous in their failings. As we age, for example, our bodies are more inclined to fail us and we are more likely to be aware of them and of the risks they incur.

In other work, which draws from Bourdieu's concepts of the habitus and cultural capital (see Chapter 2), Williams (1995) has also suggested that different social classes have different relations to their bodies which bear directly upon reflexive embodiment. Generally the educated middle classes are more compliant with the advice of health experts and thus, assumedly, reflect more upon their health in the manner Giddens suggests. Furthermore, as May and Cooper (2001) also claim, resources, including the crucial luxury of time, are significant in relation to body projects. This, too, would lead us to expect group differentiation in relation to reflexive embodiment. These claims are borne out by the evidence of large-scale health surveys (see also Chapter 9) which tend to identify differences in both health behaviours and related patterns of illness prevalence across social classes (Blaxter 1990; Tomlinson 2003).

To this list I would add that Giddens presents a peculiarly disembedded model of the agent. Norms and traditions may be under threat in contemporary society, as he suggests, but agents are still attached to one another in a variety of different types of relationship and these relations are important. To some extent Giddens (1992) recognizes this in his concept of the 'pure relationship', a concept which flags up the importance of relationships. The traditional material functions of intimate relations have been stripped away, he argues, such that their emotional aspect has become all important. This has opened up relationships to choice. We expect more, emotionally, from our relationships and we no longer 'make do' with emotionally unsatisfying relationships on account of material dependency. We go in search of emotionally more satisfying relationships. This is an interesting idea and is plausible if understood as an ideal type. However, Giddens fails to see that we are always already embedded in multiple sets of relations and networks which we cannot meaningfully be said to have chosen – for example, birth-family and work relations or relations with neighbours and members of our local community. Moreover, both these and the relations we have 'chosen', in so far as we choose any relations, are not 'out there' and separate from us. We are 'in' them and they, to a degree, are 'in' us (Mead 1967). We make decisions within relations, by talking with others, and find ourselves constrained by the power balances (see Chapter 2) they entail. And relations form us. We internalize them and they therefore shape our 'inner conversations' and constrain us from within (see Chapter 7). Reflexive embodiment is more dialogical than Giddens suggests, more socially shaped and subject to greater restrictions. We need a more networked conception of reflexive embodiment than he offers.

Finally, there is an ambiguity in Giddens's account. His detraditionalization thesis seems to suggest that traditions are eroding and that this is making room for individual decision and choice. We have to choose because there are no rules or prescriptions for us to follow. Other elements of his account, however, including his focus on risk and life politics, tend to suggest that choice is necessary because we are faced with a range of competing and conflicting prescriptions; one public voice tells us to do this, another the opposite, a third something different again and so on. In some respects these theses amount to the same thing. If there are many conflicting rules then, in effect, there is no rule. However, in terms of the concept of choice the difference is important. If we have to choose because there are no longer any guides for us to follow then we must choose without having anything to choose between. This is arguably impossible and likely to result in anomie, as Durkheim suggests. If Giddens believes that we choose in such a social vacuum then I believe his position is flawed because it presupposes choice without explaining how it is possible. If, by contrast, we have to choose because many aspects of our lives are subject to competing claims then our individual decisions are, in fact, social processes; we decide by engaging in dialogue with the competing voices in question (albeit perhaps sometimes quite brief dialogues which amount to dismissing as 'cranks' or 'boffins' those we are not inclined to follow). This may be confusing but it is not necessarily anomic because the social world offers the individual a basis upon which to choose. Moreover, choosing how to live our lives amounts to social participation because we are engaging in the debates and dialogues that shape our times, albeit perhaps in the relatively privatized space of our own 'internal conversations' (see Chapter 7). It will become apparent in future chapters that I find the latter, social model of choice in late modern societies persuasive and workable. Indeed, I believe that it is very important.

Conclusion

Whatever the limits of their respective positions, Durkheim and Giddens both raise important and similar points for our reflection upon reflexive embodiment. In the first instance they raise questions of the individual and the collective, strongly suggesting that the individual takes precedence in contemporary society but each suggesting ways in which we might think about the role of collectives. Related to this are themes of choice, identity and selfhood. Modern body work is distinct, they claim, because it is chosen by the individual, in the name of individual choice. At the same time, however, both point to what we might call 'psychopathological' possibilities. Reflexive embodiment and the society which engenders it can become problematic for individuals and damaging to their mental health, resulting in certain more extreme and damaging variants of 'body work'.

2 Civilization, informalization *and* distinction

In this chapter I continue the review begun in the previous chapter, focusing upon the work of Elias and Bourdieu. More specifically I review the concepts of the 'civilizing process', 'informalization' and 'distinction'. All three concepts are utilized in Elias's work. Bourdieu, by contrast, is discussed only in relation to 'distinction'.

The civilizing process

Elias discusses the civilizing process in an early work (Elias 1994). Here, however, I will begin with a reformulation that he offers later in his career (Elias 1996). Human behaviour, he argues, is constrained by four factors. The first two are not discussed at length. They are internal organic needs and urges, amongst which Elias includes sexual urges and the need for food, and external non-human threats, such as scarcity of food and the weather. The third and fourth factors, which are more important to his thesis, are the external controls applied to human action in social relationships, and internalized forms of control derived from them. Human beings are not isolated atoms, Elias notes. We are bound up within networks of relational interdependency, which he calls 'figurations'. And this interdependency generates a balance of power which constrains behaviour. If I depend upon you for something, for example, that gives you a lever with which to influence my action. You can threaten to withhold whatever it is I want unless I do what you want. That relationship is reversible, however, since I can refuse to do what you want unless you give me what I want. All power relationships involve interdependence and reversibility for Elias, and power is always both a property of relations, rather than individuals, and a matter of balance. Having said that, balances of power are often to the advantage of one party to a relationship. Infants influence the behaviour of their parents quite considerably, for example, because their parents love them (emotional dependence), want them to be happy and thus respond to their demands and unhappiness. But parents have many more levers at their disposal than babies do because babies are more dependent, so the balance of power is generally stacked against babies. These relations of power often enforce widely diffused norms and, as such, serve to perpetuate particular figurations and types of social order. Parents, for example, attempt to control their children's behaviour in accordance with legal and moral norms. External control is not the only way in which human conduct is constrained, however. We internalize norms and assume responsibility for controlling our own actions. The civilizing process, according to Elias's later work, consists in a gradual shift in the balance between external and internal loci of control, in favour of the latter. The hallmark of the civilizing process is the gradual replacement of external by internal controls.

We find this same claim in Elias's earlier (1994) formulations but the earlier work is centred, empirically, upon a shift in standards of manners and politeness as revealed through a comparison of etiquette books from different points in the Middle Ages and early modern period. What Elias hopes to show by way of these comparisons is both the enormous discrepancy between manners in the Middle Ages and the 1950s, when he conducted his work, and also the cumulative process whereby advances pioneered at one point in time are taken for granted and built upon at a later point in time. The civilizing process, from this point of view, is conceived as a gradual shift in standards and norms.

Many of the rules of etiquette that Elias analyses are quite shocking to the modern reader, inasmuch as it seems surprising that adult social elites, who constituted the public for etiquette books, would need them pointing out. They are very basic and obvious to the modern reader. This serves Elias's purposes because he wants to argue that we now learn in our early childhood what our society has only gradually learned over centuries. Our individual childhood socialization compresses hundreds of years of collective history. We need a historical analysis to reveal this because our socialized dispositions are deeply engrained and the earlier impulses they reshaped forgotten. Our civilized disposition seems natural to us and we have learned the lessons of civilization so well that departures from civilized norms often trigger deep and unpleasant emotional responses from us, ranging from embarrassment, through shame to disgust and anxiety.

Elias gives many examples of these transitions in manners. I will reproduce a few. In 1589 the author of the *Brunswick Court Regulations* felt it necessary to state: 'Let no one, whoever he may be, before, at or after meals, early or late, foul the staircases, corridors, or closets with urine or other filth, but go to suitable, prescribed places for such relief' (cited in Elias 1994: 107). An earlier recommendation, from another source in the fifteenth century, states: 'Before you sit down, make sure your seat has not been fouled' (cited in Elias 1994: 105). Farting was subject to similar restraint. Early advice warned against holding back, on health grounds, a qualification which was later dropped, but by 1530 the guardians of good manners were recommending that it be done as silently as possible, and covered with a cough if noise was unavoidable: 'The sound of farting, especially of those who stand on elevated ground, is horrible. One should make sacrifices with the buttocks firmly pressed together. ... simulate a cough' (cited in Elias 1994: 106). Likewise for men urinating in the proximity of women, as the *Wernigerode Court Regulations* of 1570 state: 'One should not, like rustics who have not been to court or lived among refined, honourable people, relieve oneself without shame or reserve in front of ladies, or before the doors or windows of court chambers or other rooms' (cited in Elias 1994: 107). Similarly 'obvious' prescriptions are listed for table manners, nose blowing, spitting, nudity, behaviour in the bedroom, relations between the sexes and, in particular, aggression. A decline in aggression and violence is a key aspect of the civilizing process, for Elias. We are increasingly expected to control our aggressive and other excited or emotional impulses (Elias and Dunning 1986). However, he adds that many contemporary leisure activities allow for a 'controlled decontrolling' of emotion and excitement which can serve a cathartic function in relation to the stress this generates. Many leisure activities generate 'tensions' akin to those we are expected to control in our everyday lives and allow for a controlled release of them, thus allowing us to 'let off' the 'steam' that our modern self-controlled disposition generates (Elias and Dunning 1986).

Many of the rules of civilization relate to organic needs or urges, such as eating, sex, sleep, defecation and urination. Elias (1994) notes this himself and it is an interesting aspect of his theory since it identifies a point at which organic and social processes overlap and interpenetrate. The rules of the social world increasingly control organic urges and their satisfaction, such that these urges become socially shaped, but these urges cannot be wished away. They have to be dealt with and, as such, exert their own shaping influence upon both society and individual conduct. This is an interesting contention from our point of view as it sets clear limits to our understanding of the plasticity of the body and brings the relatively autonomous organic nature of the body into focus in relation to our understanding of reflexive embodiment. Whilst the demands of civilization are social in origin, reflexive agents find themselves 'in charge' of an organic nature with impulses and needs that must be fulfilled and managed. Reflexive agents must 'referee' the contest between organic and social demands. And their organic nature may 'resist' their socially derived aspirations. The desire to lose weight by dieting must contend with hunger pangs, for example, whilst the desire to 'chisel' a body through exercise runs up against bodily fatigue, inertia and the need for rest and sleep.

As noted above, internalization of the demands of civilization has a deep impact upon personality formation in Elias's view. We do not refrain from urinating in the corridors of public buildings simply because we know that there is a rule against it. It does not occur to us to do this and it strikes us as disgusting that somebody would. And if we did accidentally wet ourselves in a public place we would feel deeply embarrassed and ashamed. This is because the civilizing process has involved a considerable reshaping of our sensibilities, a lowering of our threshold of embarrassment and shame, and it has attached these feelings to a much wider range of activities. Infants and small children provide an interesting illustration of this inasmuch as there is very little that they feel ashamed or embarrassed about, certainly with respect to such things as their natural functions and naked bodies; but they learn. Likewise with aggression: although we may still experience aggressive impulses we appear to have lost our taste for what now strike us as the more sadistic pleasures of life in the Middle Ages. We appear to have lost our taste for burning live cats, for example:

> In Paris during the sixteenth century it was one of the festive pleasures of Midsummer Day to burn alive one or two dozen cats. This ceremony was very famous. . . . a sack or basket containing the cats was hung [over a fire]. The sack or basket began to smoulder. The cats fell into the fire and were burned to death, while the crowd revelled in their caterwauling. Usually the king and queen were present. Sometimes the king or dauphin was given the honour of lighting the fire.
>
> (Elias 1994: 167)

Elias uses the term 'habitus', which he defines as a second nature imposed upon our primary biological nature, to describe these historically variable sentiments, tastes, internalized norms and the increased capacity for self-control they presuppose.

Elias is dealing with changes that are self-conscious in the short term but unintended and not available to consciousness in the long term. The civilizing process has taken place over a stretch of time that defies any individual's memory, and Elias is keen to point out that standards and behaviour patterns, once established, are taken for granted and deemed both natural and invariant. This 'forgetting' of the past is part of the process whereby we learn to feel ashamed, disgusted or embarrassed about behaviours which our ancestors (and childhood self) performed with delight and an absence of inhibition. Nevertheless, individuals are aware of changes in the shorter historical span that they live through, as adults, and to this extent reflexivity is central to the civilizing process. The writers of etiquette books seek to announce changes in fashionable society to their readership, and readers seek to self-consciously change their conduct. The original readers of the books Elias analyses were contributing to a long-term historical process they were ignorant of but they were, nevertheless, involved in a self-conscious attempt to bring their own behaviour into line with the 'new', 'more civilized' norms of fashionable society. They were reflexively embodied. In reading and applying the advice in the etiquette books they were constituting their own bodily functions and behaviours as objects of self-inspection and intervention. Moreover, Elias notes that the concept of civilization itself plays a crucial role in the civilizing process. This is not his concept, he protests. 'Civilization' and 'culture' (in the sense of 'being cultured') are social values which were and are important to the people in the various societies he studied. Individuals aim to be civilized or cultured.

What explains the civilizing process? The first important point to make in this respect is that it is a process and that Elias has a very specific conception of processes and their relation to 'society' (see Elias 1978, 1994; Elias and Dunning 1986). Society is not a 'thing' over and above individuals and their activities, for Elias, but rather exists in and through human action or rather in and through human interaction and the various networks of interdependency (figurations) that both shape this interaction and are shaped by it. Consequently society is always in process, constantly changing as agents respond to both their own past actions and the actions of others.

This process of becoming is shaped by its own history via habitus. Habitus, which may be defined at the level of either the individual or the group, are structured sediments of the past (dispositions) which shape action in the present in a manner which affords the mixture of stability and change that constitutes narrative continuity in history. Each generation acquires a language from the one preceding it, for example. They are 'programmed' by way of social immersion to speak and think in the language of their parental generation; their native language becoming second nature (habitus) to them. They will modify this language slightly, however, largely unintentionally, by way of their collective usage. And they will pass it on, in modified form, to the next generation, who will do the same. Language is therefore simultaneously reproduced and modified. So it is with norms and other cultural forms.

In addition, power balances and interests emerge within specific figurations, providing both a motive and a means for some agents to act so as to preserve their own position, lending the institutional order of society a relative stability. When the pattern of relations in society was such as to facilitate the emergence of a centralized state, advantaged in all relevant power balances with other key political players, for example, the agents of the state had both motive and means to preserve that particular aspect of the status quo. Furthermore, via a process of institutionalization their position acquires an independence and outlives them. Nevertheless, the stability of society is a matter of degree and its processual nature entails that there is always some change. Even the most routinized forms of behaviour evolve and change over time, if only by force of accidents and minor adjustments.

Conceiving of society as a process has the effect that change is not in need of explanation. It is built into the very concept of what society is. It is stability, if anything, that calls for special explanation. Nevertheless, we might want to account for specific processual trends, such as the civilizing process. Even here, Elias is cautious. In a figurational conception everything and everybody is connected to everything and everybody else (albeit sometimes at several steps removed). Each affects and is affected by its others. Within this context processes can take on a life and direction of their own but we cannot speak of their 'causes'. Causal analysis presupposes linear relations between independent and dependent variables, the former acting 'externally' upon the latter. In social life, however, elements and actors are interdependent and interacting. There is no linearity in their relationships and one cannot separate independent and dependent variables: *a* influences *b* but *b* also influences *a*. The interaction of agents may manifest a direction but that direction is an effect of the non-linear dynamics of the interaction itself. And nothing acts upon this 'system' externally since anything that affects it is also affected by it and thus forms part of it:

> [A] basic tissue resulting from many single plans and actions of men can give rise to changes and patterns that no individual person or plan has created. From this interdependence of people arises an order *sui generis*, an

order more compelling and stronger than the will and reason of the individual people composing it. It is this order of interweaving human impulses and strivings, this social order, which determines the course of historical change; it underlies the civilizing process.

(Elias 1994: 444)

Having said this, Elias's analysis points to certain key aspects within this process which have influenced its direction and persistence. One important element is the emergence of the centralized nation-state and its effective monopolization of legitimate violence. Internal warfare within the boundaries of what we now regard as nation-states was very common in the Middle Ages, as was violence more generally. As such a propensity to violence and aggression had a positive survival value and there was little in the fabric of everyday life to constitute an incentive for controlling aggression. Of course there was a level of self-control. Society is impossible without some degree of self-control and no individual will survive long without it either (Elias and Dunning 1986). There was much less need for it at this time, however, and violence and aggression had a much higher instrumental value. As the centralized nation-state emerged, however, for reasons Elias (1994) discusses at length, internal warfare was curbed and society 'pacified'. Moreover, having achieved central political control, agents of the state set about securing their position by, amongst other things, claiming exclusive rights to the use of violence (e.g. by way of the army). Internal violence threatens state power and stability so states seek to eliminate it. They prohibit unauthorized use of violence, using their own superior force if necessary. In this context the propensity towards violence and aggression serves very little purpose for the individual and is often disadvantageous, since it gets one 'into trouble'. Moreover, the capacity to control one's aggressive impulses acquires a positive instrumental value. It is better adapted to life in modern figurations. Hence, there is a social pressure towards self-control.

This point speaks primarily to the need to control violence and aggression. Self-control is, in some ways, generic for Elias, however. Learning to control one's aggressive impulses is learning to control one's impulses in general, and will have a more general impact. However, he offers at least three further theses regarding the origin and role of modern manners.

First, he links manners to expressions of deference and obedience in the pacified power relations that are increasingly common in modern societies; that is, relations where the sanctions available to the advantaged party are not generally used and have become implicit. Relations in the royal court are the key example of this. Courts were a major source of the generation of new codes of manners, particularly in France. In part this was because courts were a site where elites struggled for distinction (see below). More importantly, however, manners were a means by which members of the court both won the favour of the monarch and avoided offending him (a faux pas which might be fatal). Manners, as signs of deference, were the currency of courtly interaction. They emerged as a way of stabilizing political relationships and upholding differences in status by means other than violence.

Although he does not discuss other power relations in the same detail, it is clear that Elias believes that this same dynamic applies in other relations of power, including that between husbands and wives, parents and children, and teachers and children. In each case the stronger party can demand respect from the weaker, in the form of manners and other displays of deference, but in each case that stronger party will respond civilly, in return, as a means of teaching their subordinate by example, rewarding compliance and maintaining a pacified social relationship wherein force remains unnecessary. If everybody is polite and does what is expected of them then force is unnecessary. The rise of manners is, in this respect, closely tied to the history of pacification.

Second, as noted above, Elias discusses the role of manners and etiquette in struggles for distinction, particularly amongst rising elites from outside the aristocracy who do not have the distinction of 'blood' to fall back upon. Manners have been a crucial mechanism by which social and economic elites have sought to embody and make concrete their elevation above others in social space; to give themselves a distinct identity and an air of superiority. Moreover, such struggles can be inflationary, thereby fuelling a civilizing process. Elite manners filter into the lower ranks and are appropriated: 'what used to be distinguishing features of the upper classes are likewise spreading to society at large' (Elias 1994: 461). This undermines their distinguishing function, such that newer and more 'civilized' manners have to be devised, which again filter through and so on. This is accelerated to the degree that civilized elites both come to believe in their new civilized ethos, and thus wish to educate the 'barbarians' in the classes below, and need or want the lower orders to recognize their markers of distinction. The lower orders, who are sometimes the intended targets for displays of sophisticated demonstrations of grace, manners and so on, will not be suitably impressed unless they have learned to recognize refinement, but to the extent that they have they are already 'catching up', thus ratcheting up the baseline of civilized decorum.

Finally, Elias refers to the increasing complexity and differentiation of society. On one level what concerns him here is the generic demand for self-control in modern societies. He notes, for example, how precarious the act of walking down a busy modern street is for an individual, such as an infant, who lacks full self-control. Compared to medieval villages, modern towns are death traps which call for split-second regulation of conduct. Likewise, in a fascinating discussion of time, he observes how medieval individuals could orient their lives around the broad temporal markers of dawn and dusk, winter and summer, whilst their modern equivalent will miss their bus if they are even 30 seconds late (Elias 1992). At a further level, Elias is aware of the many different contexts in which individuals meet in modern society and, in particular, meet as strangers. Social worlds were relatively small in the past and one did not often meet strangers. In the modern world, by contrast, we meet new people all the time. Moreover, we meet people in different capacities: as workers, teachers, doctors and so on. Such interactions are potentially awkward as we share no history with strangers and have not learned what will offend or please them. There is thus a need for clear rules about interaction – a framework of manners that everyone can work within. Etiquette books have been written, in part, to meet this need and to standardize expectations. Manners substitute for the framework which shared history affords interaction, where such a framework is missing.

A note on informalization

Recently Elias's thesis has come up against a number of objections focused upon 'decivilization processes' (Mennell 1990) – that is, the possibility, fully allowed for by Elias, that the civilizing process may go into reverse. A number of aspects of modern society have been focused upon in this respect, including apparent upswings in levels of violence in inner cities and the grand violence of the Nazi Holocaust, which was unfolding as Elias was writing his original study. Here I will focus upon what has been called the 'informalization process'. This notion centres upon the observation that, since the 1960s, there has been a general relaxation of rules regarding etiquette and, for example, sexuality and nudity. Is this relaxation an indication that the civilizing process has slipped into reverse? Elias and his apologists claim not (see Wouters 1977, 1986, 1987, 2004; Mennell 1990; Elias 1996). He concedes that informalization has taken place and cites a shift in balances of power within key figurations, effected in part as a consequence of the campaigns of late twentieth-century social movements, as one of the key elements in this process. As the balance of power between husbands and wives, adults and children, teachers and pupils has shifted in the favour of the (once) subordinate, he argues, the etiquette and ritual surrounding those relations has broken down too. This is not a breakdown in the civilizing process according to Elias, however. On the contrary, he claims that the above-mentioned shift in power balances means that individuals once controlled to a greater extent from the outside are now required and expected to exercise a greater degree of self-control. In effect, informalization involves and rests upon even greater self-control, and this marks a step forward in the civilizing process. There is an example of this type of argument in *The Civilizing Process* itself. Elias (1994) notes that bathing habits and costumes are changing at his time of writing, allowing greater displays of naked flesh. Is this a sign of decivilization? He concludes that it is not, because such displays of naked flesh demand an even greater level of self-control than practices of covering up. Men are now so self-controlled that we can contain ourselves at the sight of a woman in a bathing costume!

Interestingly, in his reflections on informalization Elias develops an argument quite similar to those of Giddens (see Chapter 1). External norms are eroding, he argues, and individuals must therefore exercise more choice for themselves. They must manage themselves and their bodies in increasingly uncertain contexts.

Elias assessed

There is much in Elias's work that is impressive and persuasive. His focus upon interactions, figurations and processes is compelling, in my view, and his concept of power balances is persuasive. His openness to biology is refreshing and his focus on internal and external loci of control is interesting. Moreover, he encourages us to think about both the reflective and the pre-reflective ways in which we seek to work upon our 'bodies', casting these behaviours in the context of the overlaps of our individual (biographical) and long-term collective histories. His attempt to deflect the claim that informalization reverses the civilizing process is flawed, however. First, it involves slippage in the definition of the civilizing process. Much of the original argument for the civilizing process, as I noted above, is based upon observation of cumulative changes in standards of behaviour prescribed in etiquette books. The focus upon self-control is always evident but the changes in the etiquette books bear a large part of the burden of proof and, for much of the text, define the civilizing process. At the very least, therefore, one would have to conclude that the civilizing process involves changes in both standards and loci of control. And informalization, even if it does involve greater social control, which is questionable (see below), involves a relaxation of standards. Thus by one of Elias's criteria, at least, it constitutes 'decivilization'.

Second, the slipperiness of the argument generates contradictions in Elias's position and begs questions about meaning that he does not address. To use the bathing costume example, Elias seems to suggest that medieval women could not have walked around in modern bikinis for fear of overexciting males. Only modern men can withstand that temptation. However, elsewhere in *The Civilizing Process* he is clear that nudity was treated in a relatively matter-of-fact way in the Middle Ages. Men would have seen women naked as a matter of course but for that reason would not, in every context, have attached sexual significance to this and would not, therefore, have needed to restrain themselves. Perhaps informalization of nudity is a return to this earlier, casual attitude, a historical reversal that rests less upon self-control than upon a contextually sensitive interpretation of naked flesh. Naked flesh does not necessarily signify sexual availability and therefore does not automatically trigger a state of arousal which needs to be controlled. Conversely, concealed flesh is arousing in some contexts, especially when norms and prohibitions give it sexual significance, and may necessitate self-control if civilized order is to be maintained – see Gagnon and Simon (1973) on arousal and meaning, and Foucault (1984) on 'the repressive hypothesis'.

Third, Elias assumes that a reduction of external controls must equate with an increase in internal controls, but it is not clear that this assumption is right. At one point, for example, he notes that an increase in teenage pregnancies is an indication that young women are now expected to make their own decisions and exercise more control over their sexual and reproductive behaviour than previously, when their parents would have exercised this control (Elias 1996). I can see Elias's point, but rising levels of teenage pregnancy, not to mention rates of sexually transmitted diseases (see Figure 2.1), might equally indicate that young women and men are not exercising internal restraint, certainly not to the extent that they used to be externally restrained, and that their sexual behaviour is increasingly unregulated. By any of Elias's definitions this is decivilizing.

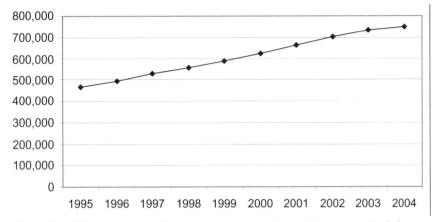

Figure 2.1   Diagnoses for all major categories of sexually transmitted disease in the UK (http://www.avert.org)

Finally, related to this, in his early formulations Elias (1994: 441–3) links internal and external controls by way of what he calls 'the social constraint towards self-constraint'. This argument suggests that self-constraint is reinforced by external controls (e.g. the threat of punishment). We control ourselves internally because we fear external sanctions. If power balances have shifted, as Elias concedes, therefore, and external controls have been removed from some groups, there is every reason to suppose that the internal controls of these groups will collapse too, resulting in decivilization. Agents no longer have a reason to control themselves to the same extent because the threat of external sanctions is removed. Informalization involves at least an element of decivilizing in my view therefore.

Returning briefly to my point about the overlap between Elias and Giddens, I believe that these points about informalization are important because they suggest that the process has freed certain domains of everyday life from normative regulation and opened them up to choice. Certain basic standards remain in place, in most contexts at most times, and levels of regulation vary across contexts, but behaviour is less normatively prescribed now than in the 1950s. It is also worth reiterating Elias's view that the 'new social movements' of the 1960s and 1970s played a central role in effecting these changes because they tipped the power balances that sustained these norms, as well as attacking the norms themselves, and encouraged experimentation with lifestyle and the body. This point connects with and deepens Giddens's (1991) reflection on 'life politics'.

Distinction

The theme of 'distinction' that emerges in Elias's account is also found elsewhere in sociological accounts relevant to an understanding of reflexive embodiment in modern society. Within early sociology, both Simmel's (1971: 294–323) account of fashion and Veblen's (1973) account of 'the leisure class' focus on attempts by aspiring groups to generate visible, embodied markers to distinguish them from those they consider beneath them. And more recently, Foucault (1984: 124) discusses the role of sexual morals in 'maintaining caste distinction' amongst the newly emerging bourgeoisie of the eighteenth century. Finally, Baudrillard (1998), in his discussion of *The Consumer Society*, a study which deems the body the ultimate consumer object, puts distinction at the heart of his analysis. The concept of distinction is most famously associated with the work of Bourdieu (1984), however. He shows how consumption and lifestyle patterns mirror patterns of class differentiation, seemingly both drawing from and reinforcing underlying class relations. Moreover, the body is central to Bourdieu's analysis.

Of some relevance here is the theme of bodily hexis – that is, the manner in which social agents embody their position in the social world in the very way in which they 'use' their bodies. We are all familiar with the differences in ways of speaking which divide social classes, particularly differences in accent. Bourdieu (1979, 1984, 1992) pushes this further, arguing that such stylistic differences extend to a range of 'uses of the body', and he extends the same analysis to gender. Sexual distinctions are embodied in acquired dispositions. There is an interesting overlap with Elias here, inasmuch as Bourdieu attributes at least some of these differences to a greater degree of self-restraint amongst the bourgeoisie and petite bourgeoisie and theorizes this in terms of habitus. Bourgeois ways of speaking and eating, he argues, involve tighter, smaller, more controlled movements of the mouth. The bourgeoisie are 'tight-lipped' and 'uptight'. This is their disposition, their attitude towards the world, and it manifests in other aspects of movement too. Furthermore, he effectively picks up Elias's (1994) historical account, arguing that the distinction by way of manners which Elias's elites were striving to establish has become deeply engrained in the enduring culture of those groups, as habitus. Manners still play an important role in differentiating the middle class and, paradoxically, naturalizing their advantage by lending them a 'natural air' of leadership and superiority. Established elites no longer need to try to mark out their distinction because their cultural 'superiority' is deep-rooted in a habitus that both functions and is reproduced without conscious intention.

Hexis is habitual, according to Bourdieu's account, to the point where it seems natural to everyone and passes between generations without effort or thought. However, he also reflects upon more deliberate 'body projects', again emphasizing class and gender differences (Bourdieu 1977). The key emphasis in his analysis is upon the way in which occupation affects an agent's relation to their body, at the level of the habitus, which in turn then affects both their propensity to engage in body projects and the types of body project in which they engage. His use of the concept of habitus, here as elsewhere, is not preclusive of an understanding of action as strategic, however. The habitus, for Bourdieu, is a pre-reflective 'feel for the game' derived from involvement in various social 'games', particularly, for example, the 'dating game' in 'marriage markets' and the 'promotion game' in the employment markets. It disposes the agent to act 'instinctively' in advantageous ways, in much the same way that a sports player will.

Bourdieu assessed

Some critics have argued that the salience of class has diminished today relative to Bourdieu's time of writing and have called for a move away from the class-based style of analysis that he offers (Pakulski and Waters 1995). I will address this criticism, empirically, later in the book. In this chapter it must suffice to make two critical points of my own. First, gender relations have changed considerably since Bourdieu's time of writing, in a manner which affects his argument. In the first instance, the notion of 'marrying age' is problematic today, not least because increasing rates of divorce and remarriage imply that a sizeable proportion of the population may marry on more than one occasion, at different (but not clearly prescribed) times in their lives, and indeed that individual marriages themselves may be less stable and known to be so for those in them. For these reasons a woman cannot 'cash in' her physical capital, once and for all, in her early twenties, even if her looks will serve no purpose for her in employment markets. In so far as looks remain important in relationships, that pressure is more constant because women are more likely to pass through a series of relationships across their lifetime. In addition, although the glass ceiling may remain for women, gender inequalities in labour markets have shifted in their favour and they are far more likely, therefore, to be financially independent. This alters the power balance and bargaining chips of men and women within relationship markets. If women do not depend upon men for money then they may demand something else in their choice of partner, including good looks. The stereotypical rich woman who takes a 'toy boy', whilst more predominant in fantasy than in actual fact, nicely captures this; she does not need a man with money, whom she must try to please, so she goes for a 'sexy bod' who pleases her in other ways. By the same token, men are in less of a position to be choosy if the demand for their goods (money) is diminished and women will feel less pressure to 'look nice for him' if they contribute the same or more to their joint finances; unless, of course, there is some reciprocation. None of this takes account of lesbian and gay relationships, moreover, which are much more prominent today than previously, and which both have their own, different dynamics, and exert an influence upon heterosexual culture. The so-called 'metrosexual', who draws aspects of body work from gay men's culture into a male heterosexual lifestyle niche and identity, is one example of the latter phenomenon.

Second, Bourdieu's theories of distinction and the pursuit of profit pose questions of meaning and motivation which his studies do not satisfactorily answer. The concept of a 'struggle for distinction' suggests intention. Bourdieu's analysis does nothing to prove intention, however. In addition, though some studies do point to 'occupational appropriateness' as a factor shaping women's body projects (Gimlin 2002; Hochschild 2003; Black 2004), Bourdieu's very economistic understanding of reflexive embodiment is not borne out at the level of meaning in any of the studies I have reviewed. Agents do not frame their body work in terms of profit and investment, except perhaps inasmuch as they view healthy behaviour as an investment in the future (but this is a matter of intrinsic goods rather than exchange values).

We should therefore be wary of doing so ourselves. Perhaps agents act in a utilitarian manner without consciously thinking so, as some rational action theorists claim (Becker 1978), but then neither Bourdieu nor rational action theorists have established that claim satisfactorily. If agents do not account for their practice as the pursuit of profit what reason do we have for arguing that this is what they are doing? Moreover, agents do not theorize their practice in terms of class. There is some evidence to suggest that hexis, manners and the 'respectability' that surrounds them form a basis for class identities, at least within fractions of the working class (Skeggs 1997; Charlesworth 2000), and certainly we have reason to believe that, for example, objective class-based differences in linguistic accents persist, but the evidence for more explicit body projects, as noted in Chapter 1, suggests that they are understood by those who practise them as manifestations of individuality rather than group belonging, with no suggestion that the former is a coded reference to the latter. Whether objective class differences manifest in this domain is discussed in Chapter 9.

Conclusion

Between them, Bourdieu and Elias identify three different social dynamics that shape reflexive embodiment and effect the diffusion of practices relating to it. First, the civilizing process is conceived as a universal process affecting all members of Western societies. Moreover, it is conceived of in terms of norms and sanctions which secure its de facto universality. We would thus expect some reflexive body practices to be universal. One of the dynamics underlying the civilizing process is the pursuit of class distinction, however. We might thus expect some reflexive bodily practices to be class-specific. Moreover, these practices are not imposed upon agents as norms but rather strategically adopted by actors pursuing status. Finally, however, the civilizing process is being undone, in part, by a countercurrent of informalization. This is creating social spaces wherein choices rather than norms steer behaviour. Choice will be shaped by many factors, of course, but in the absence of norms and sanctions actors may opt in or out of them and we would thus expect to find a cluster of reflexive body practices with a range of rates of appropriation. In brief, we can derive a differentiated picture of reflexive embodiment from the work of Elias and Bourdieu, in which different clusters of practices are characterized in different ways. In addition, Elias and Bourdieu also alert us both to the tension that is generated by attempts to mould the body, as biological and social demands clash, and to the mobile and blurred boundary between reflective and pre-reflective forms of body work. These are important developments.

3 Power, resistance *and* discipline

Elias's account introduced us to themes of self-control and power. Here I consider another writer whose work revolves around these themes: Michel Foucault. Many different aspects of Foucault's work are potentially important to us. Amongst his early studies, for example, is an account of the formation of modern medical ways of perceiving and conceptualizing the body (Foucault 1973). And in his later work we find an account of 'technologies of the self' – that is, of the various ways in which individuals, at different points in history, have elected to work upon their own bodies, behaviours, thoughts and appetites in an effort to fashion their selves in particular ways (Foucault 1987a, 1988a, 1988b, 1988c). I touch upon these works here but my main concern is with the account of 'body-power' that he posited in the middle period of his work, particularly in *Discipline and Punish*.

Technologies of power

In *Discipline and Punish* Foucault describes a fundamental transformation in 'technologies of power' within European societies which occurred around the time of the French Revolution of 1789. This transformation is graphically captured at the outset of the book by way of a comparison of two punishment regimes, separated by 80 years. The first account centres upon the public execution and torture of a regicide, Damiens, in 1757. Foucault describes how Damiens' punishment was prescribed: 'the flesh will be torn from his breasts, arms, thighs and calves with red hot pincers ... on those places poured molten lead, boiling oil' (cited in Foucault 1979: 3). In addition, his body was to be drawn, quartered and burned. In the event, however, the horses were not accustomed to quartering and his body did not break, even after two extra horses were added. As a last resort 'they were forced, in order to cut off the wretch's thighs, to sever the sinews and hack at the joints' (cited in Foucault 1979: 3). Some witnesses claimed that Damiens survived the quartering and was alive when what remained of him was thrown onto the pyre.

Foucault's second account is of a prison timetable which prescribes in great detail the expected behaviour of inmates. At the first drum roll, it stipulates, prisoners must rise and silently dress. By the second they must be dressed and have made their bed. At the third they must stand at the end of their beds and proceed to the chapel. Every aspect of their day is mapped out in this way. The contrast with the drama of Damiens' execution could not be greater. It is not merely penal practice that has changed in the 80 years separating these examples, according to Foucault, however. The timetable is just one amongst a number of new practices which start to appear in the documentation surrounding prisons at this time. More importantly, however, sifting through the manuals and plans associated with lunatic asylums, schools, factories, workhouses, army barracks and hospitals, Foucault finds references to the very same themes and practices. What has changed in this 80-year period, he argues, is the way in which people are managed and controlled across a range of contexts. A new apparatus of control has emerged, with a new modus operandi and rationale. Certain of the above institutions were new to European society in the eighteenth century. Even the older institutions were undergoing a radical reorganization, however, and the changes they were undergoing were in each case much the same. *Discipline and Punish* is an exploration of the common rationale, themes and practices that Foucault discerns in these manuals and plans.

One central theme is visibility and surveillance. In the old regime power worked by way of its visibility. The spectacle of torture and execution was a means by which the absolute monarch could demonstrate his power to the masses, showing them what would become of them if they transgressed. Castles, palaces and the grand cathedrals of the Church served the same purpose. Power works in this context by way of a display of size and force – that is, by way of its visibility. In the modern regime, by contrast, power works by making those subject to it visible – by surveillance. The architecture of power is no longer focused upon making power visible as a threat. New architectural arrangements function to make the inmates of buildings and institutions visible. This involves segmentation and, in some cases, individualization. The exercise of power is often held to deindividualize, Foucault notes, but in fact power works by separating 'the mass' into individuals, rendering each of them distinct and accountable. Partitions and cells within buildings play a crucial role here as they separate out individuals or small groups. And the manipulation of time by way of timetables plays much the same role. It specifies where in space any individual will or should be at any given time. They can be found instantly. The widespread use of timetables and of spatial/architectural partitions, which Foucault dates from this time, constitutes a key development in the societal apparatus of power therefore.

So, too, do various forms of record-keeping. In the ancient regime, Foucault notes, only the great and powerful were written about or painted in portraits. To be written about and have one's likeness recorded were signs of power and importance. Such records were celebrations of greatness. In the modern regime, by contrast, everybody is written about, photographed and logged in dossiers and files. Everybody is assigned an identity which fixes them, makes them less elusive and allows those in authority to predict their actions and categorize them.

The theme of surveillance is famously captured by Foucault in his account of the Panopticon, an eighteenth-century prison design by the British philosopher and reformer, Jeremy Bentham. The Panopticon is a circular design, with a watchtower at its centre and rows of cells around its circumference, facing inwards towards the tower. Backlighting within the cell renders its inmate visible to the tower at any time. A blind within the tower, however, prevents reciprocation. The inmate of the cell knows that he can be observed at any time but he cannot observe the inmate of the watchtower and thus does not know if he is actually being observed. Thus a constant sense of being watched is created. In this way the inmate of the cell 'becomes the principle of his own subjection' (Foucault 1979: 203). It is his own sense of being watched which constrains his action, rendering the various whips, chains and manacles that had prevailed before this time redundant. Moreover, the watchers too are watched. The Panopticon facilitates instant access to external inspectors and was intended to do so. Bentham was as much motivated by scandals regarding the mistreatment of prisoners as by anything else. The Panopticon thus illustrates the relays of surveillance which Foucault believes run through the social body. Bentham's prison was never built. In his historical research upon the architectural plans of prisons and other public buildings, however, Foucault found that it was repeatedly cited in aspirational terms. It was an ideal that shaped practice.

Another notable difference between the old and new technologies of power is that the former tended to work negatively upon the body, breaking it, torturing it and often killing the individual, where the modern regime works positively. Nature, including human nature, began to be viewed as more malleable in the eighteenth century, Foucault notes, and numerous techniques were devised for moulding it. This included both 'Taylorist' type regimes, which sought to make human activities more effective and efficient by breaking them down into components which could be 'fine-tuned', and 'behaviour modification' regimes which sought both to 'extinguish' undesirable habits and inculcate desirable ones. In addition to micro-economies of reward and punishment, such as 'token economies',[1] this often involved procedures for ranking and grading individuals, thus allowing slow learners to be separated out from more hopeful cases and providing incentives for improvement. These new technologies of power were not designed to punish individuals. They were designed to inculcate patterns of desired behaviour; to produce good workers, soldiers and pupils; to restore the mad to sanity and criminals to a lawful life. Indeed, Foucault notes that in many manuals even 'micro-penalties' were recommended to have a positive aspect. Individuals who disobeyed or failed were required to repeat correct behaviour over and over. Bad handwriting, for example, was 'punished' with handwriting practice, until a pupil got it right. In this respect, Foucault argues, disciplinary power is positive power. It creates what is desired rather than repressing what is not.

The promotion of the health of the body was important in this context too, not least as health is important to the maintenance of efficient and effective conduct. This manifests at the individual level. Many of the pedagogic manuals that Foucault consulted, for example, emphasized 'correct posture', not only as a means of maintaining efficiency in the short term but also of preserving health and thus maintaining it in the long term. In addition, however, Foucault (1984) notes that, in the nineteenth century, the health of whole populations became an issue, a development which he dubs 'bio-power'. The welfare state is the culmination of this new form of social regulation but Foucault focuses upon its precursors (Hewitt 1983).

Knowledge of both individuals and populations is crucial to these practices and Foucault argues for the co-dependency of power and knowledge. The techniques which make individuals observable for surveillance purposes, he argues, simultaneously form the basis for empirical research on human beings. Thus, for example, empirical psychiatric knowledge emerges only after procedures for sequestering and observing the mad have been put in place because it is only then that the mad are 'collected' together and rendered visible, in a controlled environment where they can be researched (Foucault 1965, 1987b; Porter 1987). In addition, he claims that social and administrative problems often frame research questions in empirical social science, whilst the various nodes of the 'carceral network' (see below) provide the 'surfaces of emergence' for social scientific knowledge (Foucault 1972). Nikolas Rose (1985), for example, notes that empirical psychology in the UK was formed around the 'problem' of 'difficult pupils' in schools. The schools served as the first psychology labs, providing the first experimental subjects, and at the same time shaped the problems that early empirical psychologists sought to address. Moreover, much of this practical empirical knowledge is guided by and serves a direct administrative purpose. The regimes of behaviour modification that Foucault writes about, for example, were fine-tuned, if not developed, within empirical psychology, and the categorical distinctions and typologies that psychology has developed have a played a crucial role in separating out the various different subgroups within a population who are likely to respond to different forms of behavioural management (see also Rose 1985, 1989). Even where the instrumental value of the knowledge is questionable, the empirical social sciences provide legitimation for intervention; if naughty or 'slow' school children are given a psychological label, for example, then intervention seems both necessary and more enlightened and humane. Related to this, the empirical social sciences are generative of many of the norms which disciplinary power orients to. Statistical norms, in the form of averages, are a frequent by-product of empirical attempts to measure individuals and populations. These statistical norms can become moral norms, however, fuelling a process of 'normalization' which eliminates diversity and difference. Attempts to identify the average IQ within a population, for example, very easily lend themselves to a problematization of those who are 'below average'. Finally, administrative needs can play a crucial role in deciding between scientific paradigms which, in all other respects, are equally deserving and attract equal levels of support. The paradigm which best fits with administrative concerns will win the backing and support which allow it to become the dominant paradigm. Again Nikolas Rose's (1985) work, particularly his discussion of the conflict between eugenic and hygienist discourses for dominance in psychology, is illustrative of this. This contest was decided on the basis of the respective administrative utility of the two approaches.

The 'map' of power that Foucault offers is quite different from that offered by many theorists, who tend to focus upon the state and/or powerful individuals. Power is not centred in or on a particular organization or individual. Rather it is dispersed across a network of institutions (schools, workplaces, barracks, hospitals etc.) which Foucault calls the 'carceral network', a network which is increasingly integrated, such that, for example, problems encountered in the school are taken up by educational psychologists and social workers, and perhaps then by psychiatrists and the police. This may serve the interests of certain elite groups, Foucault admits, and this vast network is perhaps now incorporated in the institutional complex that we call the 'state'. We should be wary of 'top down' readings, however. The state, bourgeoisie and other 'powerful' organizations and groups do not lie behind these mechanisms as their explanation. The mechanisms and their interconnection are the products of long, independent and contingent histories, and they both pre-date and constitute preconditions for the powerful state and bourgeoisie as we know them today. Power has emerged from the bottom up.

Reflexivity as self-policing?

What has this to do with reflexive embodiment? First, it is relevant because Foucault claims that the self-mastery we enjoy in relation to our bodies and our awareness of our bodies are both products of this 'investment' of the body by these technologies of control. Disciplinary regimes are, under another description, training regimes and as such they transmit powers and skills to the individual who undergoes them. In addition, the attention to bodily details required by this training raises the individual's awareness of their body. Agents become attuned to their bodies. More importantly, Foucault claims that external relations of observation and surveillance are internalized by the agent such that they become a self-policing subject:

> There is no need for arms, physical violence, material constraints. Just a gaze. An inspecting gaze which each individual under its weight will end interiorising to the point that he is his own overseer, each individual thus exercising surveillance over and against himself.
>
> (Foucault 1980: 155)

From this point of view 'reflexive embodiment' is a product of external control. The self-awareness of social agents is self-policing, induced by the internalization of external relations of observation and 'training'. It is because of this internalization of control, in Foucault's view, that modern societies have been able to do away with the more physical forms of power. Indeed one of the central arguments of *Discipline and Punish* is that liberal democracies presuppose both the carceral network and the internalization of its mechanisms of control. We can only have rights, democracy and a civilized way of life, Foucault argues, because the micro-networks of discipline secure a necessary level of compliance.

For the most part Foucault's analysis seems to be focused upon a relatively well-defined and narrow range of practices and norms, leaving open the possibility that other practices function independently of this web of power. At a number of points in his work, however, he makes more grandiose claims – for example, that muscle building, gymnastics and 'keep fit' exercising are all part of this disciplinary network (Foucault 1980: 56). Moreover, a number of those who have used his work in 'body studies' have applied his disciplinary critique to such leisure pursuits as aerobics (Lloyd 1996) and bodybuilding (Mansfield and McGinn 1993). This is a problematic over-extension of the approach, in my view, and I return to it. First, however, we must delve deeper into Foucault's approach to consider both his concept of the body and his concept of resistance.

Foucault's body

What is the status of 'the body' in Foucault's work? This is a question that has bothered a number of critics and we must briefly consider it (see Dews 1984; Levin 1989; Burkitt 1999). I believe that there are three distinct positions on 'the body' that one might infer from Foucault's work, each problematic. The first is that he has no position on the body, as such, only on 'the body'; that is, that he is interested in representations and constructions of 'the body' and 'human nature' but brackets out questions regarding their 'reality'. This would be consistent with much of his empirical work. However, it limits his usefulness from my point of view, as I am interested in the reality of reflexive embodiment. Furthermore, Foucault does not remain within the strict confines that this position entails. His account of self-policing appears to be a claim about what human beings are really like, for example (he believes that we really are disciplined and really do police ourselves), and he frequently makes claims about 'human nature', if only to attack what he takes to be dominant views of it.

This brings us to the second position. According to this position Foucault is critical of the notion of a fixed human nature, suggesting instead that human attributes vary historically, not least as an effect of technologies of control. Most sociologists would agree with a moderate version of this thesis. Research suggests that many human attributes are socially acquired and variable. Foucault's version of this thesis is sometimes so radical, however, that it becomes self-undermining. He seems to deny the idea of any invariant and biologically constituted human nature. This is problematic because, as writers such as Elias (1978) and Merleau-Ponty (1962) have noted, the plasticity and variability of human beings is species-specific and depends upon an invariant 'plastic' nature and a hard-wired capacity to both learn and innovate. These properties will have an evolutionary history but they are static across human history and necessarily so. In addition, the language that Foucault uses to describe this plasticity tends to suggest passivity and a tabula rasa model of human beings. This is problematic empirically, inasmuch as most studies of learning suggest that it involves a great deal of active involvement on behalf of the agent. It is also theoretically problematic because it begs the question of what techniques of discipline 'hook into' if the organism is entirely historical and 'blank'. It is not clear, for example, how human beings could become involved in the various 'gymnastic' regimes that Foucault identifies as a key source of bodily self-mastery and awareness if they did not already have a considerable degree of mastery and awareness (Crossley 1996, 2004a). I do not mean to deny that the social world is a source of basic human attributes. However, Foucault's techniques do not and could not operate on a tabula rasa. Moreover, as such it is clear that the acquisition of particular habits, 'body techniques' (Chapter 8) and even 'self-control' must involve interaction between the 'trainer' and the 'trained'. It is not a matter of 'imprinting', as Foucault's language often suggests. Finally, it is not evident what mechanisms of 'self-policing' and 'self-control' are supposed to be policing and controlling if human beings simply are whatever the regimes of power in a particular historical period make them. Without a 'something else', a pre-given organism which might conceivably be deemed in need of controlling and policing, the mechanisms for policing and controlling it are redundant, irrelevant and intellectually uninteresting.

This is where the third position comes in. Some readers claim to have found another position in Foucault, in which the body is a site of incoherent, competing and irrational drives and impulses (Levin 1989; Burkitt 1999). Levin, in particular, claims that there are two contradictory positions on the body in Foucault: one historicist (as described above), the other 'libidinal'. I cannot find the textual evidence to support this claim. However, if Foucault does subscribe to this model then he is wrong. As with the plasticity thesis, most sociologists would probably accept a moderate formulation. We are all aware that social control, both external and internalized, acts upon pre-existing impulses and dispositions that it controls. However, if all that we consisted of, biologically, was a 'storm' of conflicting emotions and drives then the disciplining that Foucault describes could not occur. Discipline would have nothing to 'hook into'. And society itself would not be possible as agents would lack the basic organization necessary for their coordination. In order to be 'trained' bodies must already manifest a degree of organization, consistency and agency. And everything we know about both biology and child development suggests that they are. Organic life is ordered. This may not be the order required by the social world and socialization mechanisms might be necessary to prepare the organism for social life. But the organism is not irregular and inconsistent. If it were it would not survive biologically, let alone prove capable of education into the ways of the social world.

Resistance?

Do agents not resist the power that Foucault describes? He acknowledges that they do, but much of what he writes about resistance is extremely vague and underdeveloped (see Crossley 1994: 117–22 for a more detailed discussion). Here I want to look at two versions of the concept within his work. Both illuminate aspects of his overall position and offer interesting insights for our discussion of reflexive embodiment.

The first version suggests that investment of the body by various forms of power in itself raises claims, at the level of the body, which constitute resistance. Power excites an interest in the body that it cannot itself control:

> Mastery and awareness of one's own body can be acquired only through the effect of an investment of power in the body; gymnastics, exercises, muscle building, glorification of the body beautiful. All of this belongs to the pathway leading to the desire of one's own body, by way of the insistent, persistent, meticulous work of power on the bodies of children or soldiers, the healthy bodies. But once power produces this effect, there inevitably emerge corresponding claims and affirmations, those of one's own body against power, of health against the economic system, of pleasure against the moral norms of sexuality, marriage, decency. Suddenly, what had made power strong becomes used to attack it. Power, after investing itself in the body, finds itself exposed to counter-attack in the same body.
>
> (Foucault 1980: 56)

One example of this from Foucault's work centres upon 'health'. He claims, both above and elsewhere (Foucault 1980: 166–82), that the imposition of health regimes on the population has led to a form of resistance in which agents now demand that their health-care needs are catered for. They reach a point where they take their health so seriously that they make difficult demands upon the health services that were originally deployed to encourage them to take their health more seriously (Foucault 1980: 166–82). Similarly, he notes how the invention and imposition of 'sexuality', as an identity, upon European populations in the nineteenth century generated a basis for resistance, both in the form of the sexual revolution of the 1960s and in the form of early gay rights movements (Foucault 1984). In both cases the subjects of power accepted the identity imposed upon them (i.e. 'sexual subject' or 'homosexual') and mounted a form of political resistance upon that basis, calling for open recognition and celebration of what earlier regimes of power/knowledge had identified as their essence.

This is an interesting, if underdeveloped idea. Foucault's purpose in positing it is, I believe, threefold. First, he wants to challenge the idea that power acts upon pre-constituted subjects. Homosexuality, as an identity, for example, did not pre-exist the forms of power/knowledge which seek to classify and control it. Consequently, neither did the homosexuals (qua homosexuals) who resisted that form of power. Second, as in his concept of power, he wants to reject the notion that resistance is a matter of saying 'no' to power. Resistance may continue what power has begun: for example, gay politics has involved, amongst others things, a considerable fleshing out of the gay identity which began life in a complex of power/knowledge. Third, explaining resistance in this way seems to answer the question of where resistance comes from, how it comes about, within the context of a theory where 'human beings' simply are whatever 'power' makes them. Human beings have mastery and awareness in relation to their bodies because power 'invests' them. They have desires because power stimulates these desires. They are bothered about their health, sexuality and so on because power has made them bothered about these things. They resist because power has done such a good job that they are more body-obsessed than it is able to cope with.

I disagree with Foucault on this final point. Without denying that human beings are, in some part, the product of disciplinary and training practices, it is futile, as noted above, to deny that the efficacy of those practices presupposes active agency and a variety of specifically human attributes. Moreover, the notion that power creates the basis for resistance in this way does not work. If human beings were pure 'plastic' they would do what they are trained to do and no more. The fact that they do more suggests that there is more to them, that they can rework the categories that are applied to them, redeploy the skills and attributes that they have acquired. In short, it presupposes agency. In his very final work Foucault seems to recognize this. Indeed, he seems to recognize that power itself presupposes an agent over whom it is exercised: '[power] is always a way of acting upon an acting subject or subjects by virtue of their acting or being capable of action' (Foucault 1982: 221). For the largest part of his work, however, this insight is missing.

In addition, there is a danger that resistance is tied too closely to power, such that Foucault ignores much of what is creative about it. Collective resistance, in the form of the new social movements already referred to in this book, involves more than opposition. Activists experiment and innovate with social practices and lifestyles (Melucci 1986, 1996). The praxis of social movements is generative of discourses, identities and experiences which are irreducible to whatever they are mobilizing against (Eyerman and Jamison 1991). Importantly, this applies to the various experiments with and discourses on 'the body' that have emerged within social movement contexts. Movements have contested body power and informalized various spheres of body-related practices, challenging the policing and self-policing mechanisms that operate therein, but they have also generated new ways of thinking about and acting upon the body; new modes of reflexive embodiment. Of course they have not done so *ex nihilo*. They have used wider cultural materials, but even so, much of what has been generated in this context is irreducible to its constituents. It is new. In this respect new social movements have made a genuine contribution to the cultural basis of contemporary reflexive embodiment. The modern primitives movement, which bemoans the loss of ritual and heightened bodily experience in modern societies, pioneering new forms of 'body play' and a reinvention of traditional rituals, is one good example of this (Vale and Juno 1999; Pitts 2003).

Moreover, one form of resistance can spark another. Many studies of the mobilizations of the 1960s, when the new social movements emerged, for example, show how one movement gave rise to another and then another in a generative, escalating process (McAdam 1988, 1995). Modes of critique and protest were transferred from one domain to another, along with the energy of already politicized agents. It is not only power that generates resistance, therefore. Resistance itself generates further resistance.

In addition, the 'voices' of social movements have penetrated the collective consciousness of contemporary societies, and by that means the individual consciousnesses of even those who have not been active, such that many agents feel themselves subject to competing claims and pressures in their actions. Feminism provides a good example of this (see also Chapter 4). A woman may feel herself subject to patriarchal norms, feminist counter-norms and post-feminist replies to feminism, in addition to whatever independent desires she may have. A number of studies of both cosmetic surgery and beauty salons are interesting in this respect, as they indicate the genuine debate the women have with themselves about these treatments (Davis 1995; Gimlin 2002; Black 2004). Most are aware of the feminist argument against such treatments and yet they want the treatments and feel that their desire is not simply the product of clever advertising or patriarchal pressure. In some cases one might even say that it is feminism that is experienced as the 'policing' aspect within consciousness. Women want the treatment but feel pressured to resist this desire by internalized feminist counter-norms and fear of the likely reaction from feminist peers. Whatever the precise details, however, what is evident is that consciousness is not dominated by a single controlling force, the Panopticon watchtower, but rather subject to competing claims which are effectively brought into dialogue 'within' the individual agent. There is no single norm that the women contemplating these treatments could follow. This brings us back to Giddens (1991), and not only because the women in each of the above-mentioned studies tend to account for what they do in terms of their individuality and sense of self. Some women may be disposed to listen to one of these 'voices' more than the others, but for many women there is nothing in their immediate environment, in terms of a threat of sanctions, that will force their hand. They are condemned to think it through and choose. Contestation creates a space for choice.

The second account of resistance from Foucault's work that I want to focus upon occurs in a discussion of methodology. He is replying to the objection that his description of the Panopticon is a far cry from real life in prisons:

> if I had wanted to describe real life in the prisons, I wouldn't indeed have gone to Bentham. But the fact that real life isn't the same thing as theoreticians' schemas doesn't entail that these schemas are therefore Utopian, imaginary etc. That would be to have a very impoverished notion of the real ... the elaboration of these schemas corresponds to a whole series of diverse practices and strategies ... [and] ... induce[s] a whole series of effects in the real (which isn't of course the same as saying they take the place of the real): they crystallise into institutions, they inform individual behaviour, they act as grids for the perception and evaluation of things. It is absolutely true that criminals stubbornly resisted the new disciplinary mechanism in the prison; it is absolutely correct that the actual functioning of the prisons, in the inherited building where they were established and with the governors and guards who administered them, was a witches' brew compared to the beautiful Benthamite machine.
>
> (Foucault 1981: 10)

Prisoners resist the Panopticon but so too do guards and governors, in different ways. Resistance, in this sense, involves both non-compliance and resentment on behalf of those who must live out planners' plans, as well as unforeseen and accidental obstacles which also get in the way.

The conception of resistance is unobjectionable in itself but it points to further weaknesses in Foucault's position. Specifically, it reminds us that Foucault studies plans and blueprints. His analysis is one step removed from the implementation of those plans and one step further again from whatever effects that implementation may have. These plans are part of the social world. They are real. But they are not the same thing as what they plan for. And there is good reason to believe that, though they will shape those aspects of the world that they seek to plan and design, their realization will often be far from perfect, not least because they are not imposed upon a tabula rasa social world, nor tabula rasa social agents. We should therefore be extremely cautious when Foucault and those who use his work make claims about, for example, the investment of power in the body. It would require a different type of study to those conducted by Foucault to determine how the plans he outlines are implemented and with what effects.

Foucault assessed

At a more general level the concept of resistance poses problems for Foucault on two levels. First, as with Elias's conception of the role of new social movements (see Chapter 2), there is a question whether resistance movements have not undermined the role of discipline in late modern societies. Most of the institutions in Foucault's 'carceral network' still exist and some are more pervasive than ever. But levels of formality and deference within them are greatly reduced, even relative to the standards of the early 1960s, and many of the means of control which used to operate routinely within them no longer do so, as the conservative lament for 'good old-fashioned discipline' testifies. In particular, many of the sanctions and micro-penalties that were once available in schools, factories, prisons and so on have been removed as a consequence of liberal critiques and protests.

One might respond to this that 'good old-fashioned discipline', where it has been compromised, has been replaced with softer but no less effective mechanisms of power. We do not subject individuals to micro-economies of reward and punishment any more, for example, we subject them to counsellors who listen and subtly persuade them back into line (Rose 1989). This response is problematic, however. As in Foucault's own work, there is a danger that the concept of power becomes so overextended as to become meaningless. If individuals are not brought into line by the threat, however implicit, of sanctions, then we have no basis from which to talk of power. We would be better to concede, as I noted with respect to informalization in Chapter 2, that in late modern societies the reach of the normative regulation of conduct has declined, partly as a consequence of the efforts of social movements, and more space for individual choice and decision has opened up.

This connects with my earlier point about overextending Foucault's approach. How far into the domain of reflexive embodiment do we want to push the notion of body-power? Yoga? Pilates? Jogging? Transcendental

Meditation? We could apply the framework, potentially, to all of these practices, but that is the problem. The analysis applies everywhere, so ceases to mark out anything in particular. The critical force of the concept of power is diminished. If aerobics is body-power then body-power is nothing to worry about. The reason why Foucault's analysis seems to apply across in these ways, in my view, is that he focuses upon techniques which are widespread. One can, indeed, find echoes of the techniques described in *Discipline and Punish* in contemporary discourses on 'working out'. Moreover, even where techniques are different they are still techniques and can be analysed in a Foucauldian fashion. Technique is not power in my view, however. Following Elias (1978), I suggest that power derives from a balance or rather imbalance within relations of interdependence which affords parties to those relations leverage with which to influence one another's conduct (see Chapter 2). Power is in play when my ability to bring negative sanctions to bear upon you acts as a force making you more likely to do as I say. If you cannot bring sanctions to bear upon me then you can watch me all you like from your central Panopticon watchtower. This may be irritating for me but it is not controlling. From this point of view there is a difference between schools and factories on the one hand and aerobics classes on the other. They may both involve the same techniques but there is a threat of sanctions (legal and economic) missing in the case of aerobics, which compels pupils and workers to attend schools and factories and to submit to their techniques. Of course some agents may feel compelled to work out as a result of pressures of social acceptability, such that talk of power is appropriate here (see Chapter 4). But then a political analysis of aerobics must focus on that pressure and not on the techniques of aerobics itself.

Foucault seems to concede some of this in his discussion of 'technologies of the self' – that is, techniques which agents voluntarily take up in an effort to create themselves in a particular way. His studies of these technologies focus upon the Ancient Greeks and early Christians (Foucault 1987a, 1988a, 1988b) but he concedes that his inspiration, in part, was the contemporary 'Californian cult of the self' and, in particular, Christopher Lasch's (1991) studies of *The Culture of Narcissism* (Foucault 1988c). Some contemporary Foucauldians have tended to read this back through Foucault's studies of governmentality, exploring links between self-regulation and wider social regulation (e.g. Rose 1989, 1999). This work is important and insightful but it tends to reconceptualize technologies of the self as technologies of power when, on my reading, Foucault introduced 'technologies of the self' as a way of acknowledging and exploring forms of reflexivity and self work (including body work) which are more voluntaristic, are not reducible to power and do not necessarily fit within strategies and networks of political control and governance. Foucault appears to be seeking out domains of voluntary activity which lie outside of the vast web of control that his earlier work described. Indeed, Foucault talks in some places, making clear references to modernity, of the possibility of creating one's own life as a 'work of art'. The contrast with the disciplinary moulding of the body described in his earlier work could not be more stark. And in some respects this work converges with Giddens's (1991) more existential concerns. Foucault is engaging with modes of self-creation which are, in his view, freely chosen (albeit perhaps under the influence of popular opinion and fashion).

Conclusion

Foucault describes a vast 'carceral network' of disciplinary agents and technologies that mould the body in modern societies and suggests that reflexive awareness of the body, on behalf of the individual, is an internalization of the policing function of this network. He suggests that our worries, anxieties and judgements about our bodies derive from the normalizing project of this network, and that even our basic mastery and awareness of our bodies is a product of the investment of power in our bodies. Much of what he says is impressive. We must be wary, however. Many of Foucault's more extreme claims are self-undermining and do not stand up. In addition, his detailed empirical work focuses upon discourses about practice, such as plans and blueprints, rather than the practices those discourses discourse about or their effects. Consequently, there is a huge evidence gap when Foucault speculates about self-policing subjects. The real world, as he concedes, is a 'witches brew' compared to the idealizations he studies and we should be mindful to recognize this in our appreciation of him. Finally, we should recognize that the world he describes was a world taking shape in the eighteenth century, a world which has been subject to considerable critique and dismantling since the 1960s. There are continuities but there are differences too, as Elias's (1996) notion of informalization suggests. Having said this, Foucault gives us a way of thinking about reflexive embodiment independently of political domination via his concept of 'technologies of the self' and, though this may be an underdeveloped notion, we should perhaps take it as an indication that his work does not lead us to a singular account of reflexive embodiment as political domination but perhaps rather identifies different social logics corresponding to different practices of modification and maintenance.

Note

1.   That is, regimes in which inmates are rewarded for good behaviour with tokens which they might spend in a tuck shop, and are perhaps 'fined' for bad behaviour.

4 Consumption, gender *and the* fashion–beauty complex

This chapter considers two interrelated themes that have been touched upon in previous chapters: consumer culture and gender. I take these two themes together because much of the feminist critique of reflexive embodiment has been framed in terms of a wider critique of consumer culture. Consumption and gender are both very big areas of research. There is a great deal I could say with respect to them. I have limited myself to a few key points, however, in accordance with the central aims of the book.

The chapter begins with a brief discussion of the relation between consumption and reflexive embodiment in which I consider both how the new social movements interact with consumer culture and its bodily impact, and how the ethos of consumer culture might contradict that of the civilizing process and of Foucault's 'carceral network'. Next I consider the claim that women especially are affected by the dynamics of consumer culture, before considering how certain feminist writers have applied the ideas of Foucault to female bodies in particular.

Consumer culture

The key argument with respect to the link between consumer culture and reflexive embodiment is that contemporary concerns about the body are fuelled by the dynamics of the market and capitalist expansion. To remain buoyant, capitalist markets must constantly expand, conquering new territories – a process Habermas (1987) terms 'colonisation of the lifeworld'. 'The body' is one of these new territories. Entrepreneurs have invented a whole new set of 'needs' and 'desires' in relation to the body, so the argument goes, which they duly service (e.g. Featherstone 1982). Like the social world, different regions of our bodies and bodily life have been progressively commodified and colonized. In addition, many further developments of consumer culture have reinforced this bodily focus. New sites of consumption, including bars, nightclubs, holiday destinations and shopping centres, for example, involve a culture of bodily display which, in turn, nurtures a new and heightened body consciousness. We are aware that we are on display and this makes us more conscious of ourselves and mindful of how we appear. This has been further fuelled, moreover, by the emergence and popularity of new technologies, including mirrors, cameras and videos, which present individuals with an image of their body, facilitating and encouraging bodily preoccupation, and by a cultural shift, noted by both Sennett (1976) and Featherstone (1982), linked to new sites of bodily display, in which judgements of character are now increasingly based upon outer appearance.

In addition, the mass media, which occupy a central place in consumer culture, circulate images of bodies, cultivating ideals with which audiences identify. Advertising, which is designed to cultivate changes in behaviour and desire, is an obvious example. Most forms of media, in virtue of their visual imagery, contribute to an intensified awareness of and interest in bodies, however. And written texts, where not harnessed for the same effects (e.g. discussing appearances) often reach beneath the skin, addressing but also cultivating fears and anxieties about, for example, health and sexual performance. In addition, the culture of celebrity plays a key role. The weight fluctuations of the stars, what they wear, how their look has evolved, their beauty and physical glamour, in addition to their health problems and struggles with, for example, anorexia, obesity or addiction, are key themes. Consumer culture may not have created these anxieties and desires *ex nihilo* but it amplifies them on a scale never before seen.

The other side of this is that Western societies have become increasingly affluent, such that large sections of the population, including members of a working class which previously survived on subsistence wages, now have the means to afford a range of goods and services over and above their basic needs. The working class are no longer tied so closely to the sphere of 'necessity', as Bourdieu (1984) suggests (see Chapter 2), and their consumption patterns and tastes are therefore liberated from this constraint and more diverse. Agents modify and maintain their bodies because they can afford to.

Colonization, commodification and resistance

The notion that the body is commodified and colonized connects with a number of themes that we have already considered in this book. First, commodification of the body constitutes the body, as Giddens suggests, as an object of choices. New ways of servicing and adorning the body are pioneered which we may choose between. Second, and relatedly, this helps to call the body into question, as Giddens again suggests, because new technologies and practices challenge both traditional assumptions about the body and what were previously natural, biological limitations to its cultivation. Third, as Habermas (1987) notes, colonization is integrally linked to the mobilization of the new social movements which, I have suggested, play an important role in further questioning the body and regimes of reflexive embodiment. The link between colonization and new social movements is twofold. First, the process of breaking down traditions and calling the body into question generates a context of debate which, in turn, gives rise to factions and movements. This is particularly so when debate identifies a potential which is in some way stultified or hampered by existing social arrangements or, alternatively, which raises complex moral questions. The technical possibilities for abortion and birth control illustrate this to some extent. Debates about what we should do can generate protests about what we are doing and where we are going. Second, commodification of the body has itself generated a critical reaction. The modern primitives, for example, challenge what they regard as the nullification and desensitization of the body in contemporary culture (Vale and Juno 1999; Pitts 2003). Likewise, protagonists of the 1960s counterculture sought to re-establish their relations with their bodies by way of, for example, meditation, yoga, free love and psychedelic drugs. Bodily experience in capitalist societies is alienated, repressed and inauthentic, they claimed, and they set about trying to resolve that situation (Berke 1969).

It is equally acknowledged both in these writings and the discourses of the movements in question, however, that consumer capitalism has a remarkable durability, and that critiques and alternatives are very often drawn upon as sources of inspiration which facilitate the development of new fashions, products, markets and niches. Movements can be co-opted and their innovations incorporated and used. The desire to 'return to nature', for example, living in accordance with our bodies' needs, has generated a very fruitful marketing niche. In a typically provocative claim, which echoes this point, Baudrillard (1998) argues that the body functions as a sign within consumer culture of an authentic and natural life outside of that culture. It is not outside at all in his view, however. Rather, the natural and authentic body is but another invention of consumer culture. There is no outside. This view is too extreme in my view, and as a consequence it fails to see the generative dynamic of interaction between social movements and capitalist agents characteristic of contemporary society. Nevertheless, Baudrillard has a point. Social movements can stand outside consumer culture, reconstituting the body in new and interesting ways, and sometimes endeavour to do so, but this is only ever a temporary state of affairs and must be constantly renewed, as resistance can be incorporated and used as a resource by marketers and product developers. The tussle is more or less continuous and yesterday's protest chant can very easily become today's advertising slogan. Moreover, though social movements may tap into pre-existing bodily potential which is ignored or repressed, it would be problematic to suggest that any movement has discovered the real, authentic body. It is more plausible to suggest that movements invent new ways of thinking about and practising the body.

This observation adds complexity to our picture of reflexive embodiment in social life. I have argued in previous chapters that social movements challenge certain of the norms that surround bodily life in modern societies, calling them into question. To this we can now add that they challenge certain of the bodily ideals and possibilities generated within the market and consumer culture. We must also add, however, that commodification also calls aspects of bodily life into question. Whilst conservative in some respects, consumer culture is progressive, challenging and innovative in others. Moreover, social movements, as forces of resistance, are vulnerable to incorporation and co-optation within consumer culture. Critique is often easily absorbed and neutralized such that it must be constantly regenerated and reformed if it is to maintain its vitality and resistant quality.

Asceticism and hedonism

Consumer culture further complicates our picture, moreover, in that it appears to entail an ethos which is at odds with the image of the body–society relation that we have hitherto considered. In our discussions of both the 'civilizing process' and Foucault's 'discipline' we considered the claim that the body is increasingly subject to controlling pressures and forces. Bodies and appetites are tightly regulated in modern societies, we learned. They are made to work efficiently and effectively. This literature rejoins an established sociological tradition which claims to show that modern, industrial capitalism was founded upon an ascetic ethos centred upon hard work, self-control, discipline and the deferral of gratification (e.g. Thompson 1967; Weber 1978; Marcuse 1987). The ethos of consumerism is rather different. Desires are encouraged and cultivated. We are invited to act upon impulses rather than repressing or controlling them; to 'buy now' on credit, while the offer lasts, rather than saving until we can afford to pay; and to indulge ourselves. Pleasure, play and hedonism are the names of the game.

This is interesting because it suggests that the rise of consumer culture, like the informalization process (Chapter 2), may be a countervailing tendency to that towards increased control identified by both Elias and Foucault. The agents of discipline and the civilizing process are relegated to a position where they are just one amongst a number of agents and forces competing to shape social life, which in turn leads to a more complex social configuration than either Foucault or Elias describe: a society pulled in different directions and thus perhaps more differentiated, with different domains distinguished by the degree of asceticism or hedonism expected or allowed within them. It might equally pose difficulties for agents who must live with these potentially contradictory ethics, however.

In some respects the contradiction is more apparent than real. Feath-erstone (1982), for example, notes that consumer culture celebrates 'perfect' bodies – that is, toned, tanned, slim, fit, 'sexy' bodies. He draws attention to the narcissistic pleasure of 'looking good' that characterizes consumer societies and the voyeuristic pleasure of visually consuming the good-looking bodies of others. Moreover, he notes that the cultural scripts of consumer culture explicitly link the rewards of this society with such bodily perfection: the fun on offer in consumer culture is for those who look the part and can perform. In these ways consumer culture generates incentives for the same sorts of body as are encouraged by the discipline of production, and the two spheres are married harmoniously. In other respects there is a contradiction, however. Whilst agreeing that 'sexy' bodies and bodily control are celebrated in consumer culture, for example, Susan Bordo (1993) argues that the pursuit of bodily perfection and control, both in fact and as a matter of values, is contradicted by the ethos of hedonism, generating a double bind. To put it crudely, if we eat the burgers, drink the alcopops, take the holidays and sit in front of the TVs that consumer culture offers us then we will not look like the models that we visually consume on those televisions and celebrate as an ideal. For Bordo, moreover, we risk pathology or at least unhappiness in every direction. The slim and toned ideals celebrated in consumer culture are more or less unattainable. If we try to attain them we are likely to end up either disappointed or body-obsessed and anorexic. If we focus exclusively upon the hedonistic ethos, by contrast, we risk obesity and the various health problems associated with it. There is no happy medium within this double bind, moreover. Combining asceticism and control with hedonism constitutes a form of 'bulimia': we fluctuate between control/denial and abandonment/ gratification, feeling guilty for 'blow-outs' and punishing ourselves but then ultimately consoling ourselves with another 'blow-out'. Consumer culture itself is bulimic for Bordo, rocking as it does between these contradictory ethics of asceticism and hedonism.

Whilst she overstates the case in my view, Bordo's analysis of this double bind is important. However, we must be careful how we construe hedonism and asceticism. Bordo assumes that body work is not pleasurable. This is problematic in my view. Moreover, she tends to portray consumers as 'cultural dopes' whose consumption involves no active, interpretative or reconstructive role. Ethnographic evidence paints a different picture. In my own work on gyms and working out, for example, I found that many people (myself included) enjoy it and carve out their own social world within it (Crossley 2006). As in sport, there is a pleasure to be found in physical exertion and in the reconnection with certain aspects of embodied agency that it facilitates (see also Elias and Dunning 1986; Grimshaw 1999; Monaghan 2001b Gimlin 2002). This is a pleasure that demands work and discipline and, to some extent, involves pain, but it is no less pleasurable for that. Moreover, gyms, like sports teams, generate social connections and friendships which are intrinsically valued and enjoyed, and which can become an additional incentive to work out (Crossley 2006). By the same token, many women who have beauty treatments claim to enjoy the pampering (Gimlin 2002; Black 2004). Critics of consumer culture, like Bordo, complain that it reduces the body to its exchange value; according to their analysis, body work is oriented to the generation of a product that will be valued on wider markets. In some respects, however, it is they who reduce the body to its exchange value, failing to recognize the intrinsic pleasures that attach both to the process of body work and to its end results. Moreover, they fail to see how social agents such as gym-goers, whilst perhaps not challenging 'colonization' in the manner of activists in the new social movements, nevertheless carve out pockets of meaning, value, identity, autonomy and fun for themselves in the very heart of consumer culture (e.g. in gyms). In this respect, furthermore, certain forms of pleasure seeking, associated with consumer culture, are perfectly compatible with a disciplined and regulated body. One can have fun getting fit and striving to look good.

It might be objected that this fails to address a further problem: exclusion. The bodily ideals of consumer culture, according to Featherstone (1982), for example, whilst strictly speaking inaccessible to everyone, are less accessible to some than others; as are the practices associated with this 'body cult'. The 'body in consumer culture', for example, is young and able-bodied. Moreover, as with everything in consumer culture, services are paid for and are thus more accessible to the well-off. This is surely true. However, we must again be careful not to identify, as analysts, too closely with the ideals nor to be seduced by the advertisements of consumer culture, at least not if those we are studying do not and are not. Although gym memberships are financially costly, for example, and may exclude some on this basis, the physical pleasures of the gym, referred to above, are potentially available to all people and may actually help people who do not fit with dominant bodily ideals to feel more confident 'in their bodies' (see especially Grimshaw 1999). Moreover, the gym-goers I worked with in my above-mentioned ethnography were not young, they varied in shapes and sizes, and they were not seeking to pursue abstract bodily ideals (Crossley 2006). Most, in so far as they entertained a bodily ideal, worked with a more attainable sense of what was possible for them. They were not, to reiterate, cultural dopes. More work is needed here. Exclusion is more complex and subtle in both its mechanisms and forms than we have hitherto suggested.

Gender and the fashion–beauty complex

The bodily ideals which circulate within consumer culture, Bordo continues, target women in particular. Tides are turning, she concedes. The male body is increasingly fetishised and targeted (Bordo 2001). But women remain the key target, and this is reflected in statistics regarding eating disorders. Bordo does not review these statistics, but they are consistent with her position. Men are estimated to account for only 10% of diagnoses of anorexia nervosa, for example. And prevalence rates for bulimia nervosa in developed societies are 1% and 0.1% for young women and young men, respectively (Hoek and van Hoeken 2003). Proving a link between anorexia and consumer culture is very difficult. Incidence rates (i.e. numbers of new cases within a specific period) do appear to have risen in developed societies since the 1930s, which is certainly consistent with the idea that they are explained by social changes which might include the rise of consumer culture. But such rises might be explained by other factors and the figures are extremely problematic in any case; diagnostic criteria have changed, public awareness is greater and availability of treatment has increased, to name only a few complications (Fombonne 1995; Hoek and van Hoeken 2003).

This gender dimension is developed further by Bartky (1990). Women in contemporary society, she argues, are often reduced, in both description and judgement, to certain basic characteristics of their body qua physical object – for example, their shape and their beauty. They are objects of visual scrutiny and informal 'beauty contests' in even the most mundane contexts of their everyday lives. More importantly, women learn to view themselves in this way. They learn to adopt the perspective of the other towards themselves and inspect themselves from this perspective, becoming, in Bartky's terms, 'narcissistic'. In part this is a strategic adaptation. Women know that how they look influences how they are treated and they seek to avoid negative judgements by being the first and most critical of their scrutinisers: 'Knowing that she is subject to the cold appraisal of the male connoisseur and that her life prospects may depend upon how she is seen, a woman learns to appraise herself first' (Bartky 1990: 28). More broadly, however, women internalize the norms and perspectives of both specific others in their social network and a 'generalized other' (see Chapter 7) that Bartky dubs 'the fashion–beauty complex', such that they genuinely judge themselves in terms of their appearance and genuinely despair at their failure to live up to ideals.

The fashion–beauty complex, as Bartky (1990: 39) defines it, is 'a vast system of corporations – some of which manufacture products, others services, others still information, images, and ideologies – of emblematic public personages and of sets of techniques and procedures'. In earlier times, she argues, the family and Church were the source of dominant ideals of femininity and assumed responsibility for regulating their implementation, but as these institutions have declined in influence their role has been assumed by the fashion–beauty complex. Moreover, the latter works in a very similar way to the Church. It generates a sense of shame and inferiority in relation to the body, akin to original sin, but then offers salvation and relief from those feelings. Indeed, it even suggests that the women who fall short of modern feminine and beauty norms are, in a sense, fallen and morally reproachable: ' "There are no ugly women" said Helena Rubinstein, "only lazy ones" ' (Bartky 1990: 41). Where the fashion–beauty complex differs from religion, however, is in the constant shifting of its aesthetic norms: it is a movement with which women are expected to keep up: 'Breasts are bound in one decade, padded in another. One season eyebrows are thick and heavy, the next pencil thin' (Bartky 1990: 40). There is pleasure for some women in this situation, Bartky concedes. In learning to assume the perspective of the fashion–beauty complex they learn to perceive female bodies, including their own bodies, as sources of visual pleasure. Moreover, to a limited degree the fashion–beauty complex helps them to overcome their original state of bodily 'inferiority' and thus offers relief from the pain that it causes them. This is 'repressive satisfaction', however, derived from the satisfaction of 'repressive needs'. It is a form of alienation. Women are trapped within the objectifying gaze and mindset of the fashion–beauty complex and thereby turned away from the possibilities of creativity and transcendence that might otherwise be available to them. Furthermore, many women will never reach the ideal, to their own satisfaction, and will be perpetually unhappy about their bodies. Working-class women, in particular, suffer inasmuch as they lack the resources necessary to attain contemporary ideals of femininity and beauty.

This unhappiness and self-hate is as much integral to what Bartky means by 'narcissism' as the self-love we more commonly associate with the term, if not more so. Drawing from psychoanalysis, she understands narcissism as a preoccupation with the self, and in this case specifically the body, which may be a source of either pleasurable or painful emotions for the agent in question. Narcissism is a problem, whether pleasurable or painful, from this point of view, as it prevents the agent from realizing her possibilities for freedom. It is obviously more of a problem, however, when, as Bartky suggests, it leads to great unhappiness and anxiety for many women, and psychopathology for some.

Bartky does not offer any empirical evidence to support this notion of general unhappiness regarding the body amongst the women but there is some evidence to support the idea, particularly in relation to young women. In a small-scale qualitative study, for example, Frost (2001) found body hatred to be common amongst adolescent girls. This is supported by a larger-scale survey of 900 women aged between 18 and 24 conducted by the Bread for Life Campaign (1988). Of the respondents to this survey only 25% were happy with their weight and as many as 22% claimed that they sometimes stay at home, rather than going out with friends, because of concerns about their looks; 61% said that they feel inadequate in comparison with media images of women and 20% claimed to diet most of the time. Moreover, many psychological studies point to bodily dissatisfaction and distortions of body image among women (Grogan 1999).

Foucault and feminism

The gender theme that emerges within the consumer society debate has also been framed by way of a dialogue with Foucault (Chapter 3 above; Bartky 1990; Butler 1990; Sawicki 1991; McNay 1992; Bordo 1993; Lloyd 1996). Bartky (1990) is important again here. She is critical of Foucault for ignoring both gender-specific and less institutionalized forms of discipline. Nevertheless, she suggests that he offers a powerful perspective for thinking through issues of gender. His analysis of surveillance and self-surveillance, in particular, resonates with her concern about bodily alienation and narcissism:

> The woman who checks her make-up half a dozen times a day to see if her foundation has caked or her mascara run, who worries that the wind or rain may spoil her hairdo, who looks frequently to see if her stockings have bagged at the ankle, or who, feeling fat, monitors everything she eats, has become, as surely as the inmate of the Panopticon, a self-policing subject, a self committed to a relentless self-surveillance. This self-surveillance is a form of obedience to patriarchy.
>
> (Bartky 1990: 80)

Tying insights drawn from Foucault to insights from the work of Simone de Beauvoir (1988), she argues that: 'We are born male or female, but not masculine or feminine. Femininity is an artifice, an achievement' (Bartky 1990: 65). It is an achievement that is demanded from women, however, with a threat of sanctions for non-compliance. Bartky outlines three areas in which femininity is produced, by women themselves, via the mediation of disciplinary mechanisms which operate upon them both from the outside and, as a consequence of internalization, by means of their own self-consciousness: shape, size and general configuration of the body; comportment, posture and gesture; and ornamentation of the bodily surface. Thus she discusses the monitoring and regulation of appetite, particularly during the 'bikini season' and after the 'diet busting' Christmas holidays. She discusses the inculcation of correct feminine posture and the self-policing of, for example, sitting position and walking. And she discusses the preparation and treatment of the bodily surface:

> A woman's skin must be soft, supple, hairless, and smooth; ideally, it should betray no sign of wear, experience, age, or deep thought. Hair must be removed not only from the face but from large surfaces of the body as well, from legs and thighs, an operation accomplished by shaving, buffing with fine sandpaper, or foul-smelling depilatories.
>
> (Bartky 1990: 69)

This is sometimes described as a form of self-expression, she notes, but there is, in fact, very little variation from the ideal either permitted or practised: 'at best it might be described as painting the same picture over and over again with minor variations' (Bartky 1990: 71). Furthermore, she notes that modern society has given birth to numerous forms of expertise in relation to each of her three basic domains of femininity, expertise which prescribes and provides both goals and the means of attaining them to women.

Women may feel uncomfortable 'enacting' their femininity in these ways, Bartky concedes, both in the sense of the physical discomfort caused by the various regimes and in the respect that they do not always want to perform, but multiple mechanisms exist which ensure that femininity is reproduced. On one side, for example, she notes how internalized discipline becomes a form of self-mastery and skill (e.g. of making up or cutting calories), and as such can become something that women value for themselves and are unwilling to give up. Like any social group they resist 'deskilling'. More centrally, however, she notes that since one can only be either male or female the doing of femininity becomes central to a woman's sense of identity (see also Butler 1990). If she does not do femininity then who and what is a woman to be? This is reinforced by the fact that doing femininity, and doing it well, are intimately linked to 'her sense of herself as a sexually desiring and desirable subject' (Bartky 1990: 77).

In contrast to the conception that she identifies with Foucault, however, Bartky (1990) has a much more developed sense of resistance. This is particularly clear in certain of the early papers in her book, where she describes the practices and effects of feminist 'consciousness raising'. Through consciousness raising, she notes, women learn to perceive, think and feel differently about self, other and world. There is a sense in which, in the space of their reflective consciousness at least, they can shake off certain of the fetters of patriarchal control. This point finds expression in her discussion of Foucault in the form of a discussion of the libidinal body subject, a concept which Foucault lacks but, she argues, very much needs. The female body is a source of desires, needs and sensuous experience, she argues, and as such it is inclined to 'complain' at what is done to it in the name of normative femininity. Such 'complaints' are the basic germ of later resistance projects. When women articulate their lived bodily 'complaints', instead of repressing them, they begin to fight back.

Bartky's (1990) appropriation of Foucault is one of many in recent feminist works on embodiment. Bordo (1993) also uses Foucault, for example. Butler

(1990) offers a widely cited critique of the normativity and performativity of gender. And Lloyd (1996) has analysed aerobics from a Foucauldian point of view, tracing the various forms of expertise that shape that 'disciplinary' practice. Similarly, Mansfield and McGinn (1993) look at bodybuilding and gender from a Foucauldian perspective, exploring similarities between workout schedules and the disciplinary schedules described by Foucault.

Evaluating the gender and consumer culture theses

It is difficult to deny that much body work involves consumption and thus that contemporary forms of reflexive embodiment are shaped by consumer culture and the dynamics of the market. In addition, it is important to stress that the hedonistic ethos within consumer culture, like the informalization process, generates a countercurrent to the tendencies towards control identified by Elias and Foucault. Pleasure, immediate enjoyment and letting go are extolled in certain domains of consumption. Finally, the gendering of reflexive embodiment is very strong. We should also be mindful of a number of problems in the literature we have reviewed, however.

First, we must be careful to avoid the homogenizing assumptions sometimes carried by the notion of 'consumer culture'. Marketing experts operate with sometimes quite complex typologies of different groups of consumers and market niches, and we should be at least as sophisticated as this. Different social groups, as defined by a variety of interacting variables, consume different things, in different ways, for different purposes. And advertising campaigns target specific groups. In addition, different domains of consumption arguably invite us to behave in different and contradictory ways, undermining the sense that there is a single 'right way' to live one's life. The alcoholic drinks industry, for example, whilst it must acknowledge 'responsibility' and 'healthy living', has an economic interest in cultivating identities and lifestyles which centre upon heavy drinking. It is more inclined to try to tap into our 'inner hedonist' than health promoters or the diet and exercise industries, who must acknowledge our desire to 'enjoy ourselves' but need to tap into, for example, our anxieties about health and mortality. Consumer culture is not a homogeneous entity with a uniform message and effects for all people. Furthermore, certain groups and individuals may, for a variety of reasons, be more vulnerable to particular types of message.

This point potentially has many implications for a concept of reflexive embodiment, but one very central implication is that different groups will be affected by it in different ways. The manner in which age mediates certain of the gender dynamics discussed above is an important illustration of this. Frost (2001) makes this point forcefully with respect to female 'body hatred'. She agrees that consumer culture engenders a sense of body hatred amongst women but notes that it is young women in particular who are affected, a fact reflected in diagnostic statistics for both anorexia and deliberate self-harm. It is young women in particular who are overrepresented in these figures.

There is also a danger in identifying producers and advertisers as an all-powerful force, and of overstating their capacity to manipulate our desires.

Following Elias (see Chapter 2), I suggest that we think of power as a balance of interdependence within relationships. In this case we may depend upon producers to supply what we want, and what we want may be influenced by their advertising and marketing strategies, but they depend upon us to buy their products. In some ways we are in the stronger position because we do not need, in any absolute sense, what they are offering, but they, as industries, do need to sell to us. I have observed in my ethnography of health clubs that this has an impact on the ground. Instructors who take classes are very sensitive to the wants and objections of those who take their classes, in some cases, because bad reputations spread and unpopular teachers can lose prime-time 'slots' and even their contracts. Teachers can only be 'really cruel' or impose strict discipline if this is what their clientele want and are prepared to pay for. Similarly, given the level of competition in some places and the tendency of some consumers to shop around, clubs are very keen to monitor the wants of their members and to respond accordingly. This makes health clubs very different from the disciplinary institutions discussed by Foucault (e.g. prisons and schools), whatever the other similarities in practice. Prisoners do not choose to be disciplined, cannot opt out and thus have little opportunity to shape the regimes to which they are 'subjected'. Gym-goers, diet club members and beauty product consumers can and do. The power balance is very different (see also Chapter 3).

It might be objected that economic demand for body products and services is an effect of clever marketing. Bartky, for example, suggests that women's desires are manipulated by the fashion–beauty complex. I would not deny that we are all influenced in this way but there are two weaknesses in the argument. First, to take beauty treatments as an example, historical analysis in the USA points to the existence of a thriving culture of 'home recipes' and a local 'cottage industry' pre-existing the commercialization of beauty and skin care (Peiss 1998). Before consumer culture there was a folk knowledge which fuelled desires and anxieties concerning appearance and well-being. More-over, advances in commercialized beauty culture have often had to wait for changes in consumer belief. They have not been able simply to 'manipulate' it (Peiss 1998). Finally, many of the early pioneers of beauty culture, in the USA at least, were women who sought to build upon the above-mentioned 'cottage industry'. Beauty culture was not simply imposed upon American women by powerful corporations, even if they are now in charge. It grew up from a grassroots culture. As such there is a strong case to suggest that pre-existing demand played a considerable role in its development. Second, there is a problem in assuming that consumers are easily manipulated 'cultural dopes'. Women are capable of taking a critical stance towards the beauty industry, as feminist critiques themselves illustrate, and of thinking through their decisions to buy. Moreover, these feminist critiques are widely known, so that most women are aware of them. Indeed, a number of recent studies have found that women who purchase beauty goods and services (including cosmetic surgery) are often aware of feminist critiques and consider them before purchasing (Davis 1995; Gimlin 2002; Black 2004).

Finally, without wanting to deny that advertising generates social pressure, we must be wary not to load too much explanatory power onto it. Marketing is not magic. It is just communication, and the same communication techniques fail as often as they succeed. In part this may be because they do not tap into pre-existing desires, but I believe that we need to be more sociological here. What really influences the behaviour and desire of an individual is the behaviour and desire of those around them, their 'others', both individual and generalized (see Chapter 7). The collective, as Durkheim (1965b, 1974) argued at the dawn of sociology, generates pressures which are independent of any given individual within it but which act upon those individuals. Marketing agencies are advantaged as 'individuals' in this context because of their expertise in communication, their resources and their capacity to broadcast to millions, but they are just individuals. They must deal with the collective 'as they find it', with its own relatively autonomous tendencies and dynamics. They are more likely to succeed if they 'go with the flow', much less so if they go against it. Products, services and practices do not proliferate until they 'catch on'. This sounds like a tautology, but I mean to suggest that we must be more attentive to the complex processes and dynamics of collective life and of social diffusion; that is, of the way in which the spreading of an idea can itself generate conditions which make further spread more likely, as, for example, when 'tipping points' are reached. Likewise products and practices whose diffusion has 'tipped' and achieved a 'critical mass' might prove resistant to attempts (political or commercial) to remove them, partly because they become habitual but also because critical mass generates inertia and a pressure to conform which is difficult to resist.

Conclusion

In this chapter I have examined work on both consumer culture and the gendered dimension of reflexive embodiment. It is clear that gender is a key structuring factor in relation to practices of reflexive embodiment and that many of these practices depend in various ways upon consumption. These points are indisputable. I have tried to resist the tendency, evident in some of the literature, to variously interpret consumer culture as a form of control, akin to Foucault's 'discipline', however, or to treat it as an absolute source of many practices and problems regarding 'the body'. In some ways consumer culture is a countercurrent to the austere institutional complex identified by Foucault, encouraging choice, hedonism and acting upon desire and impulse, and even where it encourages control it operates within a fundamentally different balance of power and its effects are mediated by individuals, collectives, their dynamics and desires, all of which are relatively autonomous from it. Nevertheless, I have also noted that there is a tendency for forms of political resistance, including those centred upon the body, to be drawn into consumer culture, as marketing experts draw upon it as a reserve of innovation. This may allow these forms of resistance to have some impact upon the system but they also tend to tame forms of resistance and bend them to fit the logic of production. The currents of late modern life are starting to look very complex.

Part **Two**
Rethinking reflexive embodiment

Introduction to Part Two

When considered collectively, the theories reviewed in Part One present us with a series of conflicting images of reflexive embodiment. In the first instance, for example, we have a conflict between perspectives which emphasize control and power, and those which emphasize choice. Do we elect to modify or maintain our bodies on the basis of existential and identity concerns, as Giddens suggests, or in compliance with external and internalized social pressures, as Elias, Foucault, many feminist and consumer culture theorists suggest? I suggest that the answer differs according to the specific practice we are addressing, and there is some indication that the above-mentioned theorists agree. Giddens accepts that some body maintenance is the preserve of 'administrative power', for example; Foucault acknowledges that power is resisted and also posits a notion of voluntarily chosen 'technologies of the self'; and Elias notes that social movement activism since the 1960s has 'informalized' many previously socially regulated aspects of bodily life, opening them up to individual choice. Perhaps some practices are imposed and some chosen?

These qualifications further muddy the water, however, both because Foucault's 'resistance' is not equivalent to 'existential choice' and thus adds a third possibility to our original dichotomy (practices may be neither imposed nor freely chosen but chosen in opposition to attempts at control) and because reference to 'social movements' adds a collective dimension which conflicts with the strong claims about individualization that most of the theories we have discussed make, generating a further dichotomy. Some reflexive bodily practices are collectivizing or at least connected to collectives and collective identities; others are individualizing.

Feminist theories add further complications. First, they argue that females in particular are subject to controlling influences, whilst simultaneously exemplifying the resistance that prevents us from reducing all body work to power. Second, rejoining Giddens and Durkheim, they point to forms of body work which are statistically abnormal, socially defined as symptoms of mental illness and which entail that the reflexive agent is, to a degree, out of control without being subject to the controlling influence of another – for example, the practices associated with eating disorders and deliberate self-harm. Setting aside questions regarding the precise status of these forms of reflexive embodiment, it is clear that they have specific properties and dynamics that mark them out from other practices discussed in this book and thus call for additional or different forms of explanation. At the very least the small number of individuals involved in these practices rules out the general theories we have discussed as adequate explanations. Thus, we have yet another variety of reflexive bodily practices to add to our list.

If feminists put gender into the 'pot' then Bourdieu and Elias put class into it. Where Giddens and Foucault seem to be talking about how 'we all' behave, Bourdieu and Elias challenge this 'we', arguing that societies divide into class groups whose ways of conceiving and acting upon their bodies vary. Again this introduces the prospect of collective identities, with the middle class in particular seeking to mark out their group belonging by way of perceptible signs of distinction. In addition, it further unsettles the link between body modification and control: first, because it deems modification a strategic action rather than norm-conformity; and second, because it entails that less dominated social classes are more inclined towards body work, inverting the order we would expect if body work were an effect of domination or control. Even when Bourdieu focuses upon bodily control and restraint, as when he describes the 'tight-lipped' eating techniques of the petite bourgeoisie, he is describing self-imposed constraints devised within middle-class 'tribes' to mark out their identity and difference from the proletariat. This is a way in which the petite bourgeoisie govern themselves but it lacks the sense of external imposition implied in Foucault's account of disciplinary power.

Philosophically and methodologically the respective positions of the authors I have reviewed are not only different and competing but also incompatible. Each makes different assumptions about human nature, society, knowledge and so on, and each approaches analysis and data differently. There is good reason to believe that the approaches are irreconcilable at this level. However, if we abstract, rather crudely, their empirical claims, as I have above, then there is a plausible way of reconciling their differences within a broader, superior framework. This entails recognizing that different clusters of reflexive bodily practices enjoy a different distribution in society and are differently socially embedded, such that, for example, some are freely chosen, others are enforced, some of those enforced are also resisted, some are individual, some collective, some gender-specific, others class-specific and so on.

This may sound like a weak eclectic synthesis, but I suggest a different framing. The philosopher of science, Gaston Bachelard (2002), notes that the process of refuting theories in natural science does not always lead to their rejection. It often leads to their respecification and thereby to a more complex understanding of the phenomena they purport to explain. The observation that X causes Y, for example, may later be corrected as it is discovered that this happens only under certain circumstances. Thus later scientists argue that X causes Y under conditions Z, whilst under different conditions something else happens. I am trying to propose something similar in relation to the theories reviewed in Part One. I am arguing that rather than accepting one and rejecting the rest, on the grounds that they are mutually exclusive, we should think of each as potentially instructive in certain domains but not others. My criticisms of each, outlined in Part One, still stand and I am not suggesting that we can combine whole theories in this way; they are, as noted, incompatible in important respects. But each account does offer interesting empirical insights which it makes sense to hold on to, even if we do reject most of the philosophical baggage they bring along with them and apply them only in specific areas. Reflexive embodiment in contemporary societies is vast and complex, as are those societies themselves. Different agents and processes, including those we have reviewed, pull in different directions and divide the social world into different domains. It would be silly, given this, to suppose that we have to decide whether practices of modification are chosen or imposed, collectivizing or individualizing, and so on. A much better way forward is to appreciate that theories which focus upon one of these options or another are partial theories and that our best way of resolving the apparent conflicts between their respective empirical claims is to seek to map the domain of reflexive embodiment more comprehensively, locating the various 'regions' they describe relative to one another.

This presupposes that we can identify empirically, for each theory, a cluster of practices that it accounts for. And if this is to be an interesting argument then we must seek to replace what we can now recognize as the one-dimensional theories of Foucault, Bourdieu, Giddens and so on, with a multidimensional conception of both society and the human agent. Moreover, we need a clearer conception of what is actually involved in reflexive embodiment – that is, of reflexive bodily practices. In this second part of the book I begin to establish this groundwork. In addition to offering a map of contemporary reflexive embodiment, which locates its various 'regions', I offer a preliminary theorization of the agents, practices, relations and processes it involves.

I begin, in Chapter 5, with a discussion of obesity rates in Western societies. This brief chapter is somewhat tangential to my argument but is important because obesity trends pose a prima facie challenge to all the theories discussed in Part One, with the exception of the more hedonistic interpretations of consumer culture, and because it allows us to explore important complications in the nature of reflexive embodiment. It offers an interesting route into reflexive embodiment.

Chapter 6 builds on this and seeks to further complicate our model of reflexive agency by way of a consideration of Leder's (1990) 'absent body' thesis, Merleau-Ponty's (1962) claim that our bodies become thematic for us only when we assume the perspective of the other, and certain feminist critiques of Merleau-Ponty. This discussion, which hinges upon a distinction between our lived bodily 'I' and objectified bodily 'me', is further developed in Chapter 7, which focuses upon the work of G.H. Mead. Using Mead, I postulate a multidimensional model of the reflexive agent.

Chapter 8 builds upon this by way of a discussion of what I call 'reflexive body techniques' and of the social networks which carry and diffuse them. This gives us the conception of practices called for above and begins to develop a more multidimensional picture of the societal context of reflexive embodiment, paving the way for Chapter 9, wherein this multidimensional model is explored more thoroughly. In Chapter 9, I develop my map of reflexive bodily practices, marking out the various regions that can be explained in terms of power and norms, choice, resistance and so on. Chapter 9 also discusses survey data which form the basis of this map.

5 Obesity crisis

In this chapter I begin my own exploration of reflexive embodiment. My route in is via the rising rates of obesity in most developed societies. This may sound like an odd point of departure. Obesity is not, prima facie, the result of deliberate body work and its increasing prevalence sits unhappily with an image of a society whose members are increasingly conscious of their bodies and pursuing ideals of slimness, health and control. It is for these reasons that I am focusing upon obesity, however. It runs contrary to what our theories lead us to predict, and they cannot explain it. That makes it important and interesting. It forces us to think in more detail about the nature of reflexive embodiment. I begin with a brief discussion of the obesity statistics.

Obesity 'crisis'

Rates of 'obesity' and 'overweight', defined in terms of 'body mass index'[1] (BMI), are escalating in developed societies. Figure 5.1 demonstrates the trend

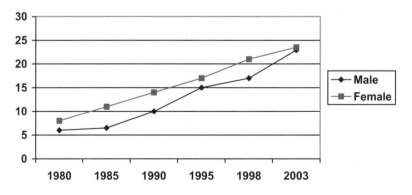

Figure 5.1 Percentage increases in obesity (BMI > 30) in England between 1980 and 2003 (National Audit Office 2001, amended with figures from Sproston and Primatesta 2004)

for England over the last 20 or so years. This rise is steeper than in many European societies and has taken England from a low to a high position on the European obesity 'league table' (Shell 2003). It is not as great as in the USA, however, and the general trend has been common throughout Europe (Shell 2003). Rising obesity levels are a recognized problem throughout the developed world.

In England, as elsewhere, the risk of obesity rises with age (see Figure 5.2). This is explained by both social and biological aspects of ageing. The current trend is affecting children too, however. The International Obesity Task Force (2005) suggests that the rise in childhood obesity is greatest in Mediterranean countries but, again, the trend is ubiquitous across developed societies. A recent report by the Royal College of Physicians *et al.* (2004) observes that obesity in 2–4-year-olds in the UK increased from 5% to 9% between 1989 and 1998, whilst rates for 6–15-year-olds more than trebled between 1990 and 2001, increasing from 5% to 16%.

The picture with respect to gender is not clear. In terms of 'obesity' UK women are marginally more affected than men. However, if we put overweight into the picture then men are much more affected. Moreover, as feminist work might lead us to expect, women are significantly more likely to fall in the ideal range (Figure 5.3). As Bourdieu suggests, however, gender interacts with class[2] (see Chapter 2). For females there is a direct correlation. Women are progressively and significantly more likely to be obese as we move from social class I through to social class V (Figure 5.4). Indeed, women in social class V are almost twice as likely to become obese as women in social class I. With males the picture is not as clear. Men in social class I are less likely to be obese than men in other social classes, four percentage points ahead of their closest rival. However, the male rate peaks in social class III (manual), and social classes II and III (non-manual) have more or less the same rates as classes IV and V, respectively. This is consistent with Bourdieu's claims, discussed in Chapter 2, that men have less work-related investment in

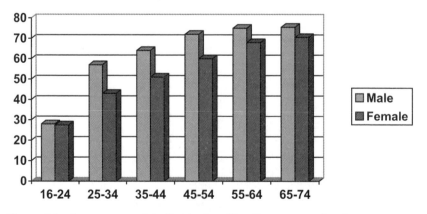

Figure 5.2 Percentage of individuals officially overweight (BMI > 25) in England in 1998, by gender and age (National Audit Office 2001)

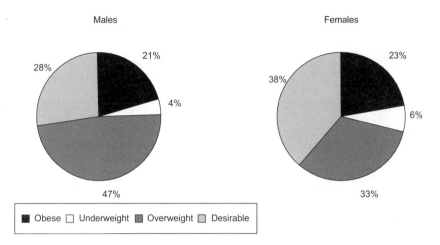

Figure 5.3 Gender and weight status in England 2001 (Sproston and Primatesta 2004)

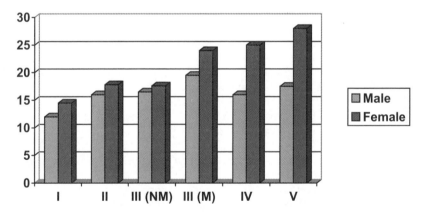

Figure 5.4 Obesity rates (percentages) by gender and class in 1998 (NM=non-manual; M=manual) (National Audit Office 2001)

physical capital, in general, but also that 'new middle class' professions, such as we find in class I, bring men into contact with discourses on health and well-being that may affect their body consciousness.

It might be argued that the obesity crisis, qua 'crisis', indicates the operation of bio-power. That we know there is a crisis, for example, points to the population-level surveillance of BMI. And the concerns of experts show just how closely our average body weight, as a society, fits into the calculations of government. Experts question whether welfare services will be able to cope with the increased levels of illness that rising obesity rates will generate and whether the economy will cope with the loss of working days through illness (e.g. National Audit Office 2001). Furthermore, the various task forces, national and international, that have formed to tackle obesity are an important example of bio-power in action. They are charged with maintaining and improving the health of national and global populations.

This is important, but I want to come at the 'crisis' from another direction: to ask how it has occurred if our bodies are subject to the level of scrutiny, regulation and intervention that the theories discussed in previous chapters suggest. Why didn't the 'police' in the carceral network and in our own subjectivities spot and prevent this crisis earlier? Aren't we all, as Giddens (1991) says, 'on a diet'? Aren't we in pursuit of the slim, sexy, tanned bodies that we find in consumer culture? Aren't we 'body-conscious' and 'fat-obsessed' to a degree never before known? The obesity crisis seems to run contrary to the claims of the theories we have examined and to challenge them.

Advocates of these theories might reply that obesity rates indicate resistance to the pressures and power identified, and thus remain consonant with them. I have argued against this claim in detail elsewhere (Crossley 2004b). For present purposes suffice it to say that the reaction of most people to putting on weight indicates surprise and disappointment, suggesting that they did not intend to become fat and were not consciously resisting the social demand for thinness. Indeed, the reaction of many people to putting on weight is to go on a diet or take up exercise. In addition, what evidence there is concerning a 'fat pride movement' gives no indication that this movement is encouraging people to become fat, as would be required if the trend is to be explained. The 'fat pride' movement serves purely to protect the rights and dignity of those who are already fat (Gimlin 2002). This leaves the possibility that fatness may be pursued unconsciously, as some feminist psychoanalysts have argued (Orbach 1985). The arguments for this claim are extremely problematic, however, even in terms of the psychoanalytic theories they draw from (see Crossley 2004b). And they both fail to explain why obesity is increasing, because they link it to allegedly static social factors, and fail to explain obesity in men, because those factors are aspects of oppression which they claim to be unique to women (Crossley 2004b). Given that we are interested in obesity trends and that women are not disproportionately represented in these trends, psychoanalytic feminism is not much help. Thus, to reiterate my point, rising obesity levels run contrary to what we would expect on the basis of most of the theories we have discussed in this book. The exceptions are those theories of consumer culture which identify its hedonistic ethos and the informalization thesis, as I explain below.

How should we understand obesity? I have argued elsewhere that the basic trend can be adequately explained only by reference to social factors (Crossley 2004b). Biological and psychological factors might explain why some individuals are more likely to become obese than others, and obesity is certainly a function of biological mechanisms and physical laws. We consume energy, in the form of food and drink, and we expend it by way of our activities. There are inputs, outputs and a ratio of input to output. Weight changes are a function of shifts in that ratio. This much is physically determined but it implies that rising obesity is an effect of a shift in the average individual's energy ratio, and social factors, particularly changes in lifestyle, are the most obvious source of that shift. Studies suggest both that we are consuming greater amounts of calorific energy, particularly in the form of food and drink that we consume outside the home, including takeaways, and that, because of the decline of paid manual labour and the use of numerous labour-saving devices, we are much less active than we once were (National Audit Office 2001). Indeed, an estimate quoted by the National Audit Office (2001) suggests that calorific output has declined over the last 50 years in the UK by an amount equivalent to running one marathon (26 miles) per week.

These are not isolated changes. They are bound up with a complex of further changes characteristic of late modern society. We now use cars instead of walking, for example, because we are regularly and frequently required to cross distances in times that would be impossible by any other means. We live further away from where we work and shop than in the past. Similarly, changes in women's patterns of working have interfered with their traditional domestic role, which has affected patterns of food preparation and eating. Specifically, families have less time to cook and more difficulties coordinating the timing of a family meal. There are too many of these factors for me to even list here, and the interaction and interdependency between them is very complex. Note, however, that they connect with some of the arguments of earlier chapters. High-calorie food and drink, and use of labour-saving devices, for example, are aspects of consumer culture. Moreover, though people may resort to labour-saving technology because late modern life makes them so busy in other respects, there is scope for interpreting their use in terms of 'hedonism'. Certainly they are 'sold' as ways of making life easier and more pleasurable. In addition, informalization may be significant. Many accounts of obesity, for example, point to the fact that major fast-food outlets target their advertising at children. Targeting children generates so-called 'pester power', which generates sales (Schlosser 2002; Gritser 2003). This explanation is important in its own right but it presupposes a shift in the power balance of the family, such that children now make their own food choices and sometimes even choose for the family. In earlier times parents controlled diet on the basis of what they deemed best for both themselves and their children. Children did not have a say. Moreover, it presupposes the breakdown of the traditional, formal family meal (see also Falk 1994). Eating practices have been informalized, not least as a consequence of a shift in the parent–child power balance that once held them in place.

Individuals are not unthinking 'molecules' in these processes. The social changes involved comprise massively complex shifts in patterns of interaction between actors who are intelligent, reflective and who know, within bounds, what they are doing. But shifts in the calorific energy ratio are unintended and unforeseen consequences of these changes. Agents have not deliberately put on weight or increased their calorie surplus. They have acted, often for good reasons, in ways which, cumulatively and unbeknown to them, have had this effect. Sometimes changes in behaviour are reflective and deliberate. Opting to drive rather than walk to work because, in increasingly flexible labour markets, one has changed job, is a deliberate if often unavoidable decision. Other times behavioural change is ushered in by way of piecemeal and practical adaptation to accidents and contingencies, becoming habitual without the agent noticing. Slipping into the habit of using the car for local trips may occur in this way. In either case, however, the agent does not notice the change in her energy ratio and, as a consequence, may very easily find herself unintentionally putting on weight.

Blind spots and episodic reflexivity

In its early stages weight gain is often not noticed by either the agent or her immediate circle. Gradual bodily changes often pass beneath the radar of reflexive consciousness because perceptual schemas and expectations change with them in a way that tracks them. Small changes effect gradual adjustments in expectations without ever being noticed. It often takes an independent, objective benchmark, whether in the form of weighing scales, a photograph or last year's bikini, to bring changes into reflective focus. Magazine confessions are replete with references to such 'shocks'. We are, in important respects, our own blind spot (see also Chapter 6), and this contributes to rising obesity because it makes it less likely that weight gain will be noticed. Weight 'creeps up' upon the unaware agent – until, that is, the above-mentioned shock moments bring it to light.

The notion of blind spots is important because it suggests that reflexive embodiment is more complex than the theories we considered in earlier chapters suggest. Self-policing and narrative self-construction are more difficult than is suggested because self-perception is obscured by blind spots. This might be overcome by regular use of weighing scales and tape measures. Rising levels of obesity suggest that most agents do not pursue this option, however. And this leads to two further critical observations with respect to the theories of reflexive embodiment that we have considered. First, the average social agent is not the self-policing, body-obsessed narcissist that some accounts suggest. I do not mean to suggest that agents are not concerned about their bodies, only that they may not be as concerned as some accounts suggest. Second, contrary to these same accounts, reflexive embodiment tends to have an episodic rather than a chronic temporal profile for many agents. Although some agents pursue body projects over years, many tend rather to be jolted into action by events which force undesirable aspects of their body into consciousness, continuing until the effect of the shock wears off and other projects become more important.

Body–society interactions

Part of my argument in this chapter is that agents shape their bodies in unintended as well as intended ways – ways that they are not reflexively aware of and may not be happy about when they come to light. Putting on weight as a consequence of changing one's lifestyle is my example. In addition, I have suggested that such body shaping is often related to the wider social world. We change our behaviour in order to accommodate changes in the behaviour of others within our networks (e.g. employers) and this, in turn, affects our body – for example, we move to a new workplace, which is further away, so we shift from walking to driving and the drop in exercise causes us to put on weight. The body, in its capacity as a biological system, is socially embedded and thus sensitive to systematic social changes. The processes of energy input and output basic to it, and, indeed, to the very definition of life itself (Smith 1986), are simultaneously social practices (e.g. eating, commuting, working in an office) and are thus shaped by changes in such practices.

Effects may pass in the other way too, however. Increases in body mass increase the probability of illness, for example, which affects both agency and reflexivity (see Chapter 6). Similarly, weight gain tends to generate unhappiness for the individual, when it comes to light, which might translate, at the collective level, into significant social trends in body work and (economic) demand for weight-loss products and services. A recent Mintel (2003) survey, for example, points to a steady rise in both the number of private health clubs in the UK and the number of members of such clubs. There was an 18% rise in the number of such clubs in the UK between 1998 and 2002 alone, with membership rising from 4.6% to 7.8% of the adult population, a 70% increase. This trend corresponds to the general claims about increased body consciousness made by the theories discussed in Part One, but one might equally claim that these figures are best explained by reference to the weight-gaining trends of late modern society. If, as I have said, changes in lifestyle are generating unintended and unwelcome weight gains within the population then one would expect to see indications that agents are trying to lose this weight. And this is what we are seeing.

This explanation is supported, qualitatively, by my aforementioned ethnographic study of a new private gym/health club (Crossley 2004a, 2006). The key reason that most agents gave for starting at the gym was that they had recently found that they had put on weight and wished to lose it; reasons for sticking at it were different and more diverse (Crossley 2006). Furthermore, the dissatisfaction that many expressed with their own bodies was usually framed by reference to their own former condition rather than abstract social norms or ideals. They claimed to want to return to how they used to be, rather than aspiring to a social or even a personal ideal (Crossley 2006). In some cases medical norms were invoked but, for the most part, this was in cases where a recent medical scare had prompted it. The body was perceived to be 'at risk' because it had faltered, not simply because that is how bodies are generally framed in late modern culture. Recent trends in health club membership might better be explained by reference to the social changes that are causing weight gain in the population, and the tension this creates between personal expectations and experiences of the body, therefore, rather than the more abstract social pressures we have discussed hitherto.

I do not mean to deny the existence of these pressures, or indeed to deny that the bodily content of self-concepts and ideals, however personalized, is shaped by a wider culture which puts such a great emphasis upon the body. But we must also recognize that 'the body' itself, as a socially embedded biological system, plays an important role in generating the reflexive 'episodes' referred to above. Body work and body projects can be triggered by unintended and unwelcome changes in the body that take the agent by surprise. This is still a sociological matter, however, and not only because body consciousness is socially shaped. As we have seen, body changes can be a direct and unintended effect of social change.

Conclusions

In this chapter I have swum against the tide a little, seeking to open up reflexive embodiment to further investigation by way of a discussion of rising obesity levels in late modern societies. This trend can be explained socially and even linked to the changes characteristic of late modern society. However, it goes against the grain of much of the theory discussed in Part One of this book, the exceptions being those theories which focus upon hedonism and informalization. The image of societies populated by self-policing or self-creating social agents has to be toned down, to say the least. Moreover, a reflection upon obesity allows us to consider: how bodies are unintentionally shaped in social life; how they can constitute a blind spot; how attention to them may be more episodic than is sometimes suggested; and how changes in the body may sometimes be a cause of reflexive body work. Reflexively embodied agents are 'in charge' of a body which may not always behave or perform as they would like, and this 'misbehaviour' needs to be factored into our accounts. Reflexive embodiment is not only shaped by the ideals, norms and practices of wider society but also by the variability of the material body itself. The next chapter seeks to build on the idea of blind spots in an effort to elucidate further the nature of reflexive embodiment.

Notes

1.   Body mass index (BMI) is calculated by dividing weight, in kilograms, by height in metres, squared. A healthy BMI is defined as between 20 and 25. Between 25 and 30 is 'overweight' and over 30 is obese. It is widely acknowledged that this measure is problematic when applied to individual cases, but it is generally deemed the most useful measure for population-level comparisons.

2.   Class, in the National Audit Office study cited here, is measured according to a six-category schema that is common in much social research. Class I consists of upper management and professionals; class II of middle/lower managers and lower stages of professional life; class IIIa of non-manual (NM), clerical workers; class IIIb of skilled manual (M) workers; Class IV of semi-skilled manual workers; and class V of unskilled manual workers.

6 Blind spots, *the* absent body *and* being-for-others

The notion of blind spots, introduced in the Chapter 5, necessitates a much more detailed examination of reflexive embodiment. We need to analyse how embodied agents access and reflect upon their embodiment. I will be offering my full account in the next chapter. Before doing this, however, I want to clear my path by elaborating further upon the notion of blind spots and discussing the idea, touched upon in relation to both Foucault (Chapter 3) and Bartky (Chapter 4), that reflexivity is mediated by way of the perspectives of others. I begin with a discussion of Leder's (1990) 'absent body', a thesis which elaborates upon the notion that the human body is its own blind spot.

The absent body

The living human body is a sensuous, perceptual-action system, according to Leder (1990; see also Merleau-Ponty 1962, 1965; Crossley 2001). It perceives and acts in the world, defining its own environment by way of its perceptions and actions. And perception and action work together, each informing and shaping the other. Under normal conditions, however, this system is largely invisible to itself. It is pre-reflexive. Perceptual consciousness is embodied. It comprises a structure of physical sensations which is generated by contact and interaction between body and world. And human beings, as those self-same bodies, *have* these sensations. However, we do not ordinarily *experience* sensations. Rather, *by way of sensations we experience a world* around us. As I stare at my computer, for example, I am having sensations but I do not perceive these sensations. I perceive the computer. The sensuous structure of consciousness is, in phenomenological parlance, 'intentional'. It is consciousness of something other than itself, of a world beyond itself. Embodied consciousness gives me a world, a setting, but in focusing upon this setting I necessarily put myself out of focus. Embodied consciousness sinks into the background of experience, allowing the world around me to be foregrounded.

The point is illustrated by situations where this arrangement is disturbed and foreground/background structures invert. When very bright lights shine in our eyes, for example, it hurts. We become aware of our perceptual sensations in the form of pain. But the price of this is that we temporarily lose our visual grip on the world. We are blinded. Bodily sensation is foregrounded in experience but external objects therefore necessarily sink into the background, where they are no longer perceived. Likewise, certain smells or tastes might make us feel sick, refocusing consciousness away from the object which makes us sick and on to the sickness itself. We no longer have a sense of bad-tasting food, rather we have a sense of our own sickness. Background becomes foreground and objects usually foregrounded recede into the background. We are all familiar with these experiences. They are not unusual. But they are distinct from our routine perceptual experience. Routinely the sensations foregrounded in these experiences reside in the background of experience such that consciousness is 'of' the world which transcends it.

I have couched this argument in terms of sensation but I might equally have focused upon perceptual organs. The eye does not see itself without the mediation of a mirror. It sees what lies before it. The nose does not smell itself and the ears do not hear themselves. Nor does the mouth taste itself; it tastes what is in it. Each organ forms a sensuous impression of the outside world but remains its own blind spot. Touch is more complex as one part of our body can touch another. However, as Merleau-Ponty (1968a) notes, even here we see the role of the foreground–background structure. When one hand touches the other we may have a sense of touching or being touched but never both simultaneously. One experience always assumes the foreground position at the expense of the other. Leder expresses this in terms of bodily absence. The body is the absent background structure of our experience, he argues, and must necessarily be so if objects within the world around us are to occupy the thematic foreground.

The body is equally absent in action. Action involves movement of the body. My current activity of typing, for example, involves movement of my fingers, arms, eyes, head and so on. This is purposive, intelligent and cultured action. To type I must know what a keyboard is and how to use it. I must know where different letters are, reaching for and tapping them in the right order. My left and right hands must work together to access upper-case letters. Indeed, my whole body must work together. If I lean back in my chair, for example, then my arms must reach further to hit the keys and my fingers must strike them from a different angle. I achieve all this without being aware of doing so, however. I know that I am typing but I do not, in any conscious or reflective sense, tell my hands to move or give them spatial instructions. I may not even know, in a reflective sense, where they are going and may not have conscious knowledge of the keyboard layout. My fingers know where to go without my having to look or search, but I could not discursively describe where individual letters are without looking or following my fingers. My knowledge of the keyboard is practical, pre-reflective and embodied. And from the point of view of my conscious experience, my body 'just moves' appropriately, without my interference (Crossley 2001). At most I become aware of how I have moved after the event; for example, when I spot a typing error. Even in such cases, however, it is not my body that I become aware of but rather the error on the screen or, more generally, in my external environment. What is true of typing is true of all action, at least in familiar situations. From the point of view of consciousness, culturally appropriate bodily action and coordination 'just happen' and, as such, fall below the threshold of perception and reflective knowledge.

Again, then, in action my embodiment manages to be largely absent from my experience. I do bodily things and my being consists in these bodily doings but my conscious is directed at the world in which I am acting rather than upon myself. I notice my own effects upon the world but am not necessarily conscious of how I generate these effects. Moreover, when we do try to concentrate upon how we do things this often decreases our competence and inhibits our action. When we become self-consciousness about how we walk, for example, we are more likely to become clumsy and awkward. Likewise, when we try to teach others practical skills we sometimes have to run through the action 'without thinking' in order to try to work out how it is that we do it. Thinking about it makes action more difficult.

Dys-appearance and bodily 'noise'

There are exceptions to bodily absence. I noted above, for example, that painful bright lights make us aware of our sensations and thus of our embodiment. Leder (1990) deems such experiences dysfunctional and labels the shifting of foreground/background structures that they involve a 'dys-appearance' of the body; that is, an appearance of the body that is brought about through its dysfunctioning. Other examples include illness and the aches and pains of ageing. When we are ill and our body does not work properly, Leder notes, we become more aware of it. Pain in particular has this effect. Likewise, as we age and find certain activities harder our body may become more noticeable to us, a focus of our experience. As our body slips into focus, however, our sensuous experiences begin to lose their intentional structure and the external world, ordinarily foregrounded in perception, slips out of focus. This is not to say that ill and old people permanently lose consciousness of the world. Individuals in extreme pain may. The pain may consume their whole consciousness. More usually, however, the focus of consciousness will fluctuate between bodily sensation and the external world. Furthermore, agents tend to limit the focus of their perceptions and actions, often unwittingly, as a way of compensating for this. They learn to habitually avoid potentially painful experiences (Goldstein 2000).

 Leder's is a philosophical argument. As I noted in Chapter 1, however, empirical work by Calnan and Williams (1991), further theorized by Williams (1995), suggests a very similar picture. They found that, if not prompted to do so, agents do not appear to spontaneously reflect upon matters of health and the body in a discussion of their everyday lives and concerns. Health and the body become reflexively thematic, they claim, when the body dys-appears through illness.

These arguments are important. They allow us to question accounts which portray self-surveillance of the body as a chronic condition in late modern societies and support my contention, in Chapter 5, that attention to the body is episodic. Moreover, in the case of Calnan and Williams, they are rooted in empirical studies of the real-life experiences of social agents and build upon a wider body of empirical studies in medical sociology which draw similar conclusions. Much of the empirical support for the theories of Giddens and Foucault, by contrast, as I noted in Chapters 1 and 3 respectively, is centred upon manuals of various kinds and thus tends to capture social ideals rather than lived realities.

In addition, the argument about the absent body is important both because it further embellishes the notion of the body as a 'blind spot' and because it raises the question of how reflexivity becomes possible. It suggests that reflexive embodiment is not a primordial condition for human beings by showing that we are, in some respects, structured in a way which makes us unaware of ourselves.

There are problems with the absent body thesis, however. Whilst it is plausible to suggest that we are unaware of our bodies in the way Leder suggests, the notion that we become aware of our bodies only through dys-appearance and illness does not ring true. For a start, it does not address aesthetic concerns about appearance – concerns which may, for some of us, be far more insistent in the course of our everyday lives than the absent body thesis suggests. There must be more to body consciousness than dys-appearance. This is partly a matter of how and why we become aware of our bodies when we do; of what triggers body consciousness. It does not take an illness to make me worry that I am ugly. It is also a matter of what we mean when we say that 'the body' is absent, however. Leder gives us an argument to suggest that what phenomenologists have called 'the lived body' or 'body-subject' is absent from experience; he suggests that we are largely unaware of, for example, the bodily basis of our actions and perceptions. And he makes a good case for this. However, when we worry about or reflect upon acne, the size of our nose, blood pressure or the risk of cancer we are not reflecting upon the lived body-subject. We are worrying about the properties of our body as an object – that is, as it appears to others, from the outside, or as it is and can be known through the concepts and procedures of various sciences, again from an external point of view. The properties of the body-as-object are not given to our immediate stream of experience any more than those of the body-as-subject. My beauty or ugliness is not felt from within, nor do the measures of blood pressure taken by the doctor necessarily correspond with anything in my experience. I can be ill without feeling ill. However, these objective properties can become thematic within reflexive consciousness and may do so independently of Leder's 'dys-appearances'. I will develop this position in what follows by way of discussion of a key contention in the work of Merleau-Ponty (1962).

Being-for-others

Leder's ideas are rooted in those of Merleau-Ponty (1962) and the arguments of the latter allow us to sharpen and extend his position. Consider the following claim:

For myself I am neither 'inquisitive', nor 'jealous', nor a 'hunchback', nor a 'civil servant'. It is often a matter of surprise that the cripple or the invalid can put up with himself. The reason is that such people are not for themselves deformed or at death's door. Until the final coma the dying man is inhabited by a consciousness, *he is all that he sees*, and enjoys this much of an outlet. Consciousness can never objectify itself into invalid consciousness or cripple consciousness, and even if the old man complains of his age or the cripple of his deformity, they can do so only by *comparing themselves with others, or seeing themselves through the eyes of others*, that is, by taking a statistical and objective view of themselves ...

(Merleau-Ponty 1962: 434; emphasis added)

Merleau-Ponty might appear to contradict Leder here. Wouldn't the body of the 'cripple', to use Merleau-Ponty's unfortunate term, dys-appear and become visible in the way that Leder's ill and ageing bodies do? In so far as ageing or disability involve aches and pains they must make the body dys-appear. That does not mean that the individual will necessarily experience their body as old or disabled, for reasons I discuss shortly. But they will be aware of their body as a consequence of such experiences. I do not think that Merleau-Ponty would disagree with this. He is making a different point. He is drawing a distinction between internal and external experiences of the body – that is, between my 'experience' of my body and your experience of my body. We have already said that 'my body' is absent from my experience, a background structure rather than a foreground object. This is what Merleau-Ponty is getting at when he claims that the dying man 'is all that he sees'. The body of the dying man is an invisible background structure which projects him into the world and what he is conscious of is the world, not his dying body. Merleau-Ponty is extending the point, however, by observing that bodies have a range of properties when viewed from the outside, as objects, by other people, that have no correlate at the level of the internal experience of the embodied agent, even when the body dys-appears. Ageing and disability are bad examples because they can involve aches and pains but Merleau-Ponty could have used the example of having two legs or two eyes. What is it like to have two legs? Two eyes? We do not know what it is like to have two legs or two eyes, partly because these properties belong to the absent background structure of our embodied experience of the world but also because we have nothing within our own experience with which to contrast this state of affairs. Having two legs and two eyes structures our experience of the world but unless we lose an eye or a leg we will never know, experientially, how it does so or indeed that it does so. There is nothing in the nature of my everyday experience that reveals its binocularity or bipedalism. Similarly, if I had been born with one eye and one leg, assuming that everyone around me was in the same position, I would not be aware that I 'only' had one of each or that my vision and movement were affected. There would be no 'only' about it, nor indeed any sense that my experience was 'affected' or diminished, since one-legged monocularity would be the experientially absent background structure of my experience and there would be nothing to compare it against. The same applies to a range of bodily experiences. My experience may be structured by my biological sex, for example, but if it is I cannot know this 'internally' because 'internally' I do not experience my experience, I experience the world around me. And in any case I lack the comparative reference point which would allow me to judge my experience or some aspect of it 'male'. To judge my experience 'male' I would need to compare it with female experiences and the experiences of other males, neither of which are available internally within my own consciousness as they are, by definition, others' experiences.

We may argue, contra Merleau-Ponty, that age is slightly different. On one level there is nothing in my experience that directly reveals my age to me. I no more feel 37 than I feel two-legged. However, my lived experience manifests a temporality that allows me to experience changes and, in particular, the bodily deterioration that goes with ageing. Perhaps I experience certain physical activities not only as 'hard' but as 'harder than they used to be'. My body dys-appears in the form of breathlessness or aches and pains, but at the same time my tacit sense of my own capacities is challenged. I do not match up to my own expectations, which are rooted in prior experience, and I therefore experience my difficulties as deterioration. Of course my failings may not be due to age. They may be due to illness. Furthermore, treating them as a matter of age requires that I step outside of my lived experience and apply socially based objective and external criteria to myself – that is, age categories and measurements. Without the concepts of age and ageing I would not experience my aches and pains in this way. This is a general point; social representations play an important role in the way in which we 'read' our bodies and experiences and thus reflexive embodiment presupposes the acquisition of these representations and their structuring role. However, as noted, my aches and pains do have a temporal structure to them; physical tasks, to reiterate, are not just hard but harder than they used to be. And there is good reason to believe that the social category of ageing owes its origin, in some part, to the sharing and comparing of such lived experiences. We have a concept of ageing and its effects because we all experience physical activity as 'harder than it used to be' over time, and we discuss this common experience in a manner which allows us to deduce its probable cause (for a similar argument with respect to the concept of disease and pathology, see Canguilhem 1998). More generally, however, Merleau-Ponty's point is borne out. There are any number of properties of the body-object, that is, the body viewed from an external position, which do not register, in the first instance, within the perspective of the body-subject, even if they contribute to the shaping of that perspective.

The implication of this position is that to experience oneself as, for example, 'crippled', indeed to experience oneself at all, one must adopt an external point of view in relation to oneself. If I am 'crippled' only from an external point of view then my sense of myself as crippled presupposes my access to this point of view. But how is this possible? How can I have an external view of myself? As he indicates in the above passage, Merleau-Ponty believes that we achieve this perspective by learning to see ourselves 'through the eyes of others' (1962: 434). I explore this in more detail in the next chapter. For present purposes, however, I will prepare the way with a brief discussion of difference and 'the look'.

Difference

Iris Young (2005) has used the work of Merleau-Ponty to develop a feminist account of female embodiment. Her engagement with Merleau-Ponty, whilst it accepts and appropriates much, is critical, however. She argues that his account of what Leder calls the absence of the body in everyday experience, and particularly the easy relationship this suggests between body and self, betrays a peculiarly male experience. The female body, she argues, is objectified to a much greater degree than the male body within popular culture and is constituted as an object of visible scrutiny in many everyday situations. Indeed, the female body is vulnerable to both unwanted visual attention and sometimes unwanted physical contact and touching. This, she argues, makes women much more conscious of their bodies and inhibits their action. The body cannot be absent from women's experience in the way that it can for men. Women have to be conscious of how their bodies look, what is visible or exposed and what accessible when they move, and this inhibits their movement. As noted above, it can be very difficult to perform an action whilst trying to think about it. The thought process seemingly inhibits the behavioural process. Moreover, women have to move in ways which minimize their vulnerability. This both further inhibits their movement in its own right and increases self-consciousness, causing further inhibition again.

This argument draws from a celebrated account of 'the look' by Sartre (1969). Feeling that we are being looked at by others, Sartre claims, changes our whole way of being. It makes us self-conscious. In the absence of this feeling we may involve ourselves in a situation to a point whereby we 'forget' or 'lose' ourselves. We become completely 'absorbed' in the situation or in our train of thought and imagination. We are, to use Leder's (1990) expression, absent from our own experience. Indications of the presence of others who may be watching us, such as a creaking floorboard or movement in our peripheral vision, quickly snap us out of this absorption, however, and make us very aware of ourselves, to the point of inhibiting our action. This self-consciousness is a form of alienation, for Sartre, because what we are aware of is not simply ourselves but rather our existence as an object of experience for another person. We do not 'belong' to ourselves because they are watching us and we are captured up in their experience. Young accepts this argument but argues that such alienation is far more common for women because women are more likely in our society to be positioned as objects of visual consumption. This is not simply a matter of being in the company of others. Men are often in the company of others. Men, however, are more often recognized as fellow subjects in such encounters and are not positioned as objects of visual contemplation. They are, for example, less often ogled. Interpersonal encounters, as Merleau-Ponty (1962) argues, are always communicative. We cannot help communicating with others. But what is often communicated to women is a refusal to engage with them as communicative subjects and a tendency rather to consume them as visual objects. Men are recognized as communicative subjects, women are constituted as visual objects.

In many respects Young is making the same point as Bartky (1990), whose ideas we discussed in Chapter 4. In both cases women's relations with their own bodies are said to be inhibited and alienated by a socially induced awareness of the body, an awareness that others, particularly men, are watching and judging them, and perhaps deriving voyeuristic pleasure from the experience. Women are conscious of the consciousness that others have of their bodies, and their own consciousness of their bodies derives from their assumption of the perspective of the other. As Bartky (1990: 38) puts it in her own analysis: 'The gaze of the Other is internalized so that I myself become at once seer and seen.'

In a more recent paper Young (1998) has argued that the situation for women has improved since she first postulated her argument. Moreover, Grimshaw (1999) has argued that, though it is most often women whose bodies are inhibited and alienated, there is a contextual aspect to this. In some contexts, she argues, it can be men who are aware of and awkward in relation to their bodies. She gives the example of aerobics. Challenging the argument that aerobics is necessarily a form of patriarchal body-power, she argues that it can be empowering for women, giving them a sense of control in and possession of their bodies. Men, however, often feel out of place in aerobics classes, in her view, and their actions are often awkward as a consequence. They feel self-conscious about acting in one of the few female spaces in contemporary society.

A similar argument to that of Young has been made by Fanon (1986) in relation to black men. The bodies of black men are subject to close visual scrutiny for a variety of reasons, Fanon argues, and this makes black men acutely conscious of themselves and their embodied presence in a variety of situations. As such, it inhibits their movement. Their bodies are not quite so absent for them nor are they at ease in their bodies in the way Merleau-Ponty suggests.

The arguments of Young, Bartky and Fanon are interesting, plausible and important. They add much to our understanding of reflexive embodiment. As with the quote from Merleau-Ponty discussed above, however, they beg the question of just how agents are able to experience themselves from the 'perspective of the other'. In the next chapter I will introduce a theory which answers this question.

A tale of two bodies?

The key conclusion of this brief chapter is that the 'body' we are conscious of in our reflexive projects is our body as perceived externally and available to other people. We are not, excepting circumstances of dys-appearance, thematically conscious of our bodies from within. The lived body is absent, experientially, in much of our experience and the body we are aware of as our own is an 'object' that we know from the outside, by adopting the perspectives of others towards ourselves. In the next chapter, borrowing G.H. Mead's terminology, I will refer to these 'two bodies' as the bodily 'I' and the bodily 'me' respectively: the bodily 'I' is the body-as-subject, the body which perceives and acts but remains 'absent' in experience; the bodily 'me' is the body as objectified in consciousness, known to others and known to itself as known or potentially knowable to others. Moreover, I will use Mead's work to address the key question that emerges from this discussion: namely, how are we able to experience our bodies as experienced by others? How can we experience ourselves from the outside? For the moment it must suffice to note that this claim, that my consciousness of my body is rooted in the perspective of others, entails that reflexive consciousness and reflexively embodiment are necessarily socially rooted. There is no 'bodily Me', no sense of my own body, in the absence of the perspectives of others.

7 I, me *and the* other

Chapter 6 concluded with the claim that we become aware of our bodies as objects by learning to perceive ourselves 'through the eyes of others'. In this chapter, drawing upon the work of George Herbert Mead (1967), I consider how we learn to perform this feat and acquire the disposition to do so routinely. Mead has a particularly persuasive vision of selfhood, reflexivity and agency which I am going to take as a central reference point in my rethinking of reflexive embodiment. Moreover, his work allows us to overcome a problematic dichotomy in the literature discussed earlier (see the Introduction to Part Two). On one side of this dichotomy is Giddens (1991), whose conception of reflexive embodiment is infused with a strong sense of agency and of the existential lifeworld of the agent but who conceives of the agent in a peculiarly atomistic fashion (see Chapter 1). On the other side are Foucault and many feminists, for whom reflexivity amounts to self-policing and political domination, with very little room for agency or genuine choice (Chapters 3 and 4). Durkheim, Elias and Bourdieu fall between these problematic extremes but none has a developed conception of the reflexive agent so they cannot really help us resolve it (Chapters 1 and 2). Mead can. I begin with a brief assessment of Mead's relation to this dichotomy before offering a more general discussion of his position.

Reflexivity, social relations and internal conversations

The isolated individual is a myth for Mead. We are always already involved in social relations and networks. The evolutionary history of our species has been shaped by selection pressures arising from collective life (see also Hirst and Wooley 1982) and our 'incompleteness' at birth makes us dependent upon others for an extended period. We grow within another's body and are born into a social group. More importantly, our capacity for thought, reflection and reflexivity emerges from an internalization of the perspective of others (see below) such that even our most private and intimate reflections engage with the other. Thought, for Mead, is an *internal conversation*; that is, a silent or subvocal conversation that we have with ourselves, in which we play the roles of different interlocutors, generally modelled on people we know, making points, responding to them, replying to responses or making further responses and so on (see also Archer 2000, 2003).

In the latter respect Mead's position anticipates Foucault's concern with self-policing. The individual assumes the observational and judgemental position of others in relation to herself. In contrast to Foucault, however, Mead understands the impact of the perspectives of others, internalized or external, in dialogical terms. We are aware of what others think or will think about our actions, for Mead, and we anticipate their responses to our actions in imaginative rehearsals of possible lines of action, but we can argue back within this imaginary space, and if we can construct a persuasive reply to what we believe will be their criticism, or can persuade ourselves that we are not bothered by what they will say and do, then we may pursue our desired course of action, either as we originally intended it or in a way modified so as to minimize the sanctions we expect to receive. Our relations with others are dialogical and the culture into which we are socialized involves 'tools' of argument, alongside prescribed norms and values – tools which we can appropriate and use to challenge those norms and ideals if, and to the extent that, we disagree with them. In some situations we may obey norms, even norms that unfairly disadvantage us, without awareness of doing so. Reflexivity and self-knowledge are far from perfect. In other cases the anticipation of sanctions that others may bring to bear suffices to persuade us to comply in spite of our opposition. Our relations with others, qua relations, involve interdependency and thus a balance of power, and when we are disadvantaged in such balances our liberty is restricted. Power balances vary across our relations and social contexts, however, and we enjoy some room to manoeuvre in most contexts.

In addition, Mead's position allows for what we might call 'poly vocal' internal dialogues; that is to say, from Mead's point of view we may bring numerous perspectives to bear within our internal dialogues, if we have internalized them. Our experience is not dominated by a single overpowering authority figure, such as Foucault's Panopticon. Thus, it may be that a woman contemplating a beauty treatment will reflect not only upon what the advertisers of the product say but also upon feminist critiques of 'the beauty myth' (Wolf 1991), post-feminist critiques of that critique, the views of her friends and so on. She may contemplate her position from a wide range of different points of view, bringing these points of view into dialogue within her own decision-making process; always assuming that she does not simply act on impulse, without thought, which is also possible according to Mead's perspective.

Dialogues of this kind are potentially creative. New views and positions emerge out of the interplay of older ones. Debate can be generative. And it can be unpredictable. As Gadamer (1989: 383) notes, 'nobody knows in advance what will "come out" of a conversation'. The pull and push of different voices could go in different directions and the conversational trajectory is sensitive both to initial starting conditions and to sometimes quite minor perturbations. A tangential suggestion might send a debate in a very new and different direction. As a dialogical being, therefore, the reflexive agent is potentially innovative and may, in the context of either real dialogues with others or imagined dialogues with their internalized representatives, sow the seeds of new cultural forms.

Mead's view upon perspectives and their internalization also poses a challenge to Bourdieu's position. In an interesting footnote in *Outline of a Theory of Practice*, Bourdieu (1979: 233, n. 16) observes that life in modern cities unsettles the taken-for-granted feel of the world which the habitus otherwise furnishes, as agents are constantly coming into contact with others (often immigrants) who have a different lifestyle and culture from their own. This observation sits unhappily with the rest of his work, where agents are said to live naïvely within their own habitual perspective, taking it for granted. It captures Mead's sense of modern life perfectly, however. For him, perspectives are constantly coming into contact, affording agents a new viewpoint on themselves and generating hybrid cultural forms which can never achieve complete taken-for-grantedness. We are creatures of habit, for Mead, but we are equally conversational agents and our conversational tendencies, whilst rooted in habit, tend to disturb at least some of our sedimented repertoires of action, bringing them into view for us. We appropriate aspects of the perspectives of others, examining our own perspective from this vantage point and thereby relativizing both. Tradition and culture or habitus lose some of their grip by virtue of our awareness of them and of their relativity (see also Crossley 2001).

I do not mean to suggest that we should drop the concept of the habitus or that Mead's work is incompatible with it. There is a strong and sophisticated sense of habit in Mead's work, and a fortiori in the tradition to which he belongs (Dewey 1988), comparable in meaning to the habitus concept. And I have argued elsewhere that reflexivity, in the manner of Mead, should be thought of as an acquired disposition or habit in itself (Crossley 2001, 2003). We have reflexive habits or a reflexive habitus. However, I am suggesting that we cannot load all of our agency into the pre-reflective domain of the habitus as Bourdieu often seems to do; that we must credit agents with greater reflexive powers than he seems prepared to grant them, if only because social change and geographical mobility have the effect of constantly unsettling assumptions and habits, and drawing diverse communities into contact with one another.

In an interesting way then, Mead emphasizes agency and reflexivity, like Giddens, but combines this with an equally strong emphasis upon social embedding, akin to that of Foucault and Bourdieu. It is for this reason that his perspective affords us an opportunity to pass between these extremes, combining their strengths whilst avoiding their weaknesses. Agents are multiply socially embedded, for Mead, and these relations shape the agents' reflexivity. They do not necessarily subordinate the agent, however. They are 'voices' in reflexive and potentially critical conversations. There are limits to Mead's perspective too. We cannot simply substitute his perspective for that of Bourdieu or Foucault because he misses much that they bring to light (partly because he was writing in the early twentieth century). We need to hold on to what is positive about their respective contributions too. But it is my contention that we can locate Mead's reflexive agent within the account we are building, in an effort to resolve some of the problems that the other theories raise. In essence, then, I am looking to Mead, in this chapter, to help me to construct a robust account of reflexive agency and thereby reflexive embodiment. I turn now to his account of the genesis of the self.

Self and other

Infants do not seem able to take an outside view upon themselves. They act and speak, when able to, in ways which suggest that they are not aware that other people have a distinct and different point of view, and integral to this is an apparent lack of awareness of the fact that they are experienced by others. Piaget (1961) refers to this as 'egocentrism', which is apt in one sense but also potentially misleading as what the child lacks, from Mead's point of view, and Piaget's, is a developed sense of self. They tend to confuse their view of the world with the world itself and, as such, fail to properly grasp the particularity of their own experience. It is only by grasping that their view of the world is just one view of the world that they will arrive at a sense of the boundaries of their own experience and thus of the very existence of their experience as a distinct thing; that is, of themselves. Recognizing that other people have a different view of the world and are distinct sites of experience is integral to this. Other people are the different vantage points on the world that allow the infant to recognize that her own view of the world is just one view amongst many. Furthermore, recognizing that they exist as an object in the experience of other people, for Mead, is what allows them to begin to experience their own self, including their own body, as an object. We are able to look upon our self, including our body, as an object, he argues, when and to the extent that we can adopt the perspective of 'the other'. Mead agrees with Merleau-Ponty, then, that we can perceive ourselves only 'through the eyes of others'. How do infants achieve this?

The first step, according to Mead, is taken during play. Infants play at being other people, taken from real life, books or television. This might begin with very simple imitation of acts that they see others perform, but it gradually grows more sophisticated such that, for example, they switch back and forth between roles and assign roles to either friends or toys. When they embark upon such play, to reiterate, they are not aware of the perspectives of others. They are merely acting out the behaviours and relationships that are visible to them in their situation, perhaps as a way of making sense of those behaviours and relationships. In doing this, however, they begin to appreciate that people play different roles and to acquire, through role play, a sense of the different vantage points and perspectives attached to those roles. Playing 'dad' or 'teacher' offers a glimpse of how the world looks from another point of view and reality thereby takes on a different, multi-perspectival complexion. Furthermore, by implication children learn that their own perspective is one amongst others. Their experience and perspective is decentred and thereby becomes recognizable as their own. They cease to conflate their view of the world with the world itself.

This is advanced, Mead continues, in so far as children play out their relationship with significant others and relive significant events within this context. They may, for example, explain the dangers of the world to themselves (or a teddy bear) as their mum explains it to them or they may scold themselves for doing something that they have previously been scolded for. They may call out 'No!' or 'ah, ah' as they perform behaviours they have been told not to do. In doing this they learn to apply the perspective of the other to themselves and thereby internalize that perspective, coming to understand themselves from the point of view of the other. The perspective of the other takes up residence within their habitus.

It is this same process of role play, moreover, which lays the foundations for the above-mentioned *inner conversation*. Just as our ability to read quietly and to ourselves is based upon our earlier acquired ability to read out loud, so too the discrete, silent and internal conversations of adult life are founded upon these earlier, more explicit dramatic performances. Moreover, role play continues in adult life and is often deployed for purposes of increasing empathy or developing self. In addition to actors, who sometimes report seeing the world differently when they have 'got into' a character, for example, 'swapping roles' is sometimes deployed as a way of allowing social actors to come to appreciate one another's point of view. And we all rehearse or replay important interactions in our imagination, getting a feel for significant others in those situations and thereby subjecting ourselves to an internalized representation of their perspective. The experience of infants is different inasmuch as they do not know what effect role playing will have, are not doing it in order to learn about other perspectives, and start from a position of 'egocentric' unawareness. But the discovery of the perspective of the other, achieved by playing roles, is much the same.

Language and linguistic categories are also important in these processes. Self-awareness emerges within a symbolic, primarily linguistic environment, and significant others, usually parents, play a key role in teaching the infant language. Moreover, they name the world for the infant, identifying objects for her, including herself. They give her and teach her to use personal pronouns (I, me, you, us) and they both individualize her, in their interactions with her, conveying a sense of her own uniqueness to her and 'mirror' back a reflection of herelf to herself. The infant acquires a sense of herself by learning to play the roles of others but she also learns to play the role of herself, to rise out of her infantile egocentrism and take up the position of a unique individual in a social world. In this respect she also begins to acquire an identity or identities; that is, a sense of who she is in the world by virtue of what she is, who she is related to and how.

The infant is not passive in this respect and her concept of self is not devoid of affect. Cooley (1902), whose work is closely related to that of Mead, stresses the role of self-feelings in the early development of the self – for example, noting how the learning of personal pronouns tends to coincide with an infant learning that she is a cause in the world (i.e. that she makes things happen), with the 'joy' that accompanies this observation and with early appropriative urges. Children learn to say 'mine', for example, as they tussle to keep hold of objects they want. These appropriative urges are early forms of a sense of self, for Cooley. Moreover, on his interpretation they illustrate the flexible boundaries of the self. The self is, in some respects, what belongs to me and what I have 'me', 'my' or 'mine' feelings about. As such it extends beyond the boundaries of my organism. Its boundaries are neither unlimited nor determined by the infant alone. They are negotiated within social interaction. The infant will assert but will also have to learn what is 'mine' and thus 'me'.

The generalized other

As children grow older, having been shaped by play, Mead continues, they are able to engage in 'games'; that is, forms of play which involve multiple players, perhaps teams and certainly rules. As with role play, game playing develops by degrees. Children begin with simple games, acquiring the dispositions that allow them to move on to more complex games. Games further develop the sense of self acquired by way of play. Where playing at being 'dad' allows children to see themselves as their dad sees them and to internalize his particular perspective, playing games demands that children see themselves from multiple perspectives at once and from the point of view of the abstract rule structure of the game. This, Mead argues, is a preparation for living in a wider society where one will be expected to live within the structure of beliefs, norms and so on of a community. However, while it induces a sense of fairness, rules, grace in defeat and so on, game play also encourages a strategic disposition. 'Playing the game' is not a matter of unthinking conformity. Players second-guess their others in order to win.

At this point Mead introduces a distinction between particular others, such as teachers or individual family members, and what he calls 'the generalized other'. The application of the concept of the generalized other has been a source of contention amongst Mead scholars. I share Blumer's (2004) view, however, that there can be many 'generalized others' corresponding both to the different communities to which an individual might belong and to successive levels of abstraction, generality and universality. Some generalized others are collectively incorporated in 'even more generalized others'.

Integral to this generalized other, moreover, is the ability of the agent to apply objective social criteria, measures and concepts to both the world and herself. Learning to play 'games' is learning to step outside of particularistic criteria of judgement and to apply criteria that are intersubjectively agreed upon. This may be a matter of accepting when a goal is a goal in football but it applies equally to the numerous standardized measures we learn to apply to our own bodily life, from age, through height and weight to blood pressure and blood sugar level. How things seem to me may not be how they seem to the majority of others, that is, to society, and internalizing the perspective of the generalized other involves learning and accommodating to this fact.

What Mead is saying with respect to the generalized other and our capacity to assume its role has much in common with a number of perspectives on the internalization of social control that I discussed in earlier chapters: specifically those of Elias, Foucault and Bartky. The 'fashion–beauty complex', 'carceral network', 'civilized norms' and 'consumer culture' are all, in certain respects, examples of a generalized other that the agent may learn to assume and apply to their self. As noted above, however, internalization does not guarantee compliance, in Mead's view. Knowing the view of the generalized other is not sufficient to guarantee my compliance unless an imbalance of power and threat of sanctions force my hand.

The bodily me

Play and games decentre an agent's experience, giving them a sense of their particularity and their existence within the experience of other people. They learn that there are external perspectives to be had upon them. Moreover, by assuming the roles of others they learn to occupy these roles, in imagination, and thereby to develop a perspective upon themselves. They become an object for themselves, as they are for others, because they assume the role of the other. This process splits the agent into two 'phases' which Mead refers to as 'I' and 'me'. In reflecting upon herself the agent is both a reflecting subject (I) and an object of reflection (me). Mead conceives of this split as temporal. He is not suggesting that subjectivity consists of two spatial 'parts'. The me emerges when the I turns back upon itself, to reflect upon itself. The I never quite coincides with itself in this process, Mead argues, and self-reflection is always historical, therefore. The agent can reflect about herself but she cannot simultaneously reflect upon her reflection, partly because she cannot do two things at once (i.e. reflect and reflect upon her reflection), partly because a second-order reflection (i.e. reflection upon reflection) must have something to reflect upon and thus must come after that which it reflects upon. In so far as it assumes a reflexive posture, therefore, the I always reflects upon a historical reconstruction of itself; that is, upon 'me':

> As given, [the self] is a 'me', but it is a me that was an 'I' at an earlier time. If you ask, then, where directly in your own experience the 'I' comes in, the answer is that it comes in as a historical figure [i.e. a 'me'].
>
> (Mead 1967: 174)

History, in this context, might be a matter of microseconds but there is a gap nonetheless and it is important because it means that the I, the agent in the present tense, is elusive. It only ever knows itself through the mode of historical reconstruction; that is, as 'me'. This maps quite closely onto what Leder (1990) argues about the absent body (see Chapter 6). The embodied I is not thematic in its own experience because it is the necessary background structure of that experience. It is absent.

Some critics have argued that Mead's position is limited in the respect that the 'me' exists in the past tense only (Wiley 1994; Archer 2000). What, they have asked, of the future? I read Mead differently. In claiming that the me exists 'in the past tense' Mead is not ignorant of the fact that we can and do project possible future selves, a 'future me'. However, an agent can only project into their own future if she already has a sense of her own self to project; that is, of 'me'. There must be a 'me' who is going to do this or be that. And this sense of me necessarily derives from the past because, as we have seen, my present being is elusive and absent, whilst my future being is hypothetical and does not yet exist. I can only exist for myself as an agent who has acted, in the past. It is important to add, moreover, that anticipation, and thus futurity, is integral to Mead's conception of action and is the *raison d'être* for his interest in role taking and selfhood. He believes that playing the role of the other allows us to anticipate how others will react to possible actions on our behalf, which in turn allows us both to weigh up whether the actions are worth it and to design those actions to elicit the most favourable of possible responses. Our grasp of our past is central to our control of our future – that is, to our agency.

Assuming the perspective of others gives us a sense of ourselves, including a sense of our body and what we should do with it. We experience our bodies as public objects and learn to tend and attend to our bodies in the way that others do. This might mean, as Bartky (1990) notes, that we learn to judge our bodies before others have the chance, and more harshly, in order to pre-empt their criticisms. It might mean, as Elias (1994) notes, that we learn to view certain of our bodily functions, products and parts as private or dirty, developing a sense of embarrassment or shame in relation to them. In both cases our body exists for us, as a thematic object, via our awareness of its existence for others.

Our bodies may be constituted as different types of object for us, in accordance with the different people we interact with, different types of relations we enter into and different practices involved. The care and love generally shown by parents to the bodies of their children, for example, constitutes the child's body, for the child, as a vulnerable and precious object to be cared for and looked after, and also perhaps cleaned and generally maintained. Children are encouraged, when leaving their parents' control, to 'eat properly' and 'wash behind your ears'. In relations with peers, by contrast, bodies take on an aesthetic and sexual meaning. They are expected to look cool and sexy. They might also be expected to perform well on the sports field, the dance floor and in bed. Taking the perspective of the other, agents learn to perceive their body in this way and to make corresponding judgements of value. These meanings are communicated through language and symbols, but also reinforced through play, games and practices. As children take over the practices by which their parents have cared for their bodies – for example, beginning to wash their own hair, clean their own teeth and so on – they actively constitute and thus come to experience their body as a vulnerable object of care. Taking on a caring role by assuming responsibility for practices of care constitutes the me differently for the I. Likewise when, in later life, they dance or dress for a night out they put themselves into a role which, in turn, constitutes their bodily me for them as an object of sexual attraction. The meaning of the me is embedded in practice (see also Chapter 8).

There is a certain dynamism here, as feedback on self and body are relayed to the agent in her interactions with others, as Cooley (1902) suggests in his concept of the 'looking glass self'. We constantly reflect back images of self to one another, directly and indirectly, in ordinary social interaction, and these reflections enter into our senses of our bodily self or me. It is difficult to sustain a sense of oneself as beautiful, for example, if others tell us or treat us as if we are not. I do not mean to present an image of selfhood as a passive reflection of the judgements of others. Agents can be resilient to negative feedback and disparaging of flattery, as Cooley noted (although this in itself may relate to a strong sense of self developed through positive relationships in childhood). Feedback regarding the self may need to be reiterated from numerous sources, including sources the agent deems authoritative, in different contexts, before the agent takes them seriously (Cooley 1902). Moreover, as Cooley argues, individuals select, to some extent, the others whose views are important to them and even then interpret and (re)construct the feedback they receive (Franks and Gecas 1992). Finally, agents are actively involved in the process of managing the impressions others have of them by way of self-presentation, as Goffman (1959) famously argues. The views and feedback of others are important, however, particularly as our body is a blind spot (see Chapters 5 and 6), and we desire the recognition of others (see below). It is difficult for an individual to get an objective sense of their own body without the reflections of their self mirrored back by others, and they know this. They are aware of their blind spots and partiality. Furthermore, it is difficult not to be affected or bothered by the views of significant others.

Relatedly, we achieve our sense(s) of our body by way of comparison with others. If others are shorter than us we feel tall. If they are thinner than us we feel fat. If they are faster than us we feel slow. This is often revealed in instances where we change reference group. My image of myself as a fast runner, supported by the fact that I can outrun all of my peers, will suffer a blow if I join a running club whose other members are much faster than me, for example. Such examples sound trivial but they illustrate that our sense of our embodied self derives from social life and experience and is not therefore internal or intrinsic. Moreover, note that comparing ourselves with others presupposes an ability to take the perspective of the other. I do not see my 'shortness' immediately in the taller people around me. I must adopt their lofty perspective to see myself as short.

Within contemporary society the sense of the me as a bodily being is, as the theorists of consumer culture argue (see Chapter 4), greatly enhanced by the wide availability of mirrors and other technical devices, such as photographs and video technology, which reflect back images of our bodily exterior to us (Featherstone 1982). These technologies constitute the bodily me as an object of visual consumption for the embodied, perceiving I. We must be careful to avoid technological reductionism in our understanding of this process, however. Mirrors and cameras are used by social agents and their effects are mediated by their use. I will illustrate this with reference to mirrors, but similar arguments apply to all technologies. In the first instance note that we have to learn to see ourselves in mirrors, as infants, usually with the mediating help of our parents. At one level this is a matter of learning what we look like and acquiring habitual familiarity with our own image, as we do images of others, a process which has been illustrated in rare instances where, for example, prisoners of war have not seen a mirror image for many years and struggle in a group situation to find their own image in the mirror. At another level it involves learning to treat the mirror as a reflective surface and the image as a 'mere reflection' of self rather than a real other (Merleau-Ponty

1968b). Use of the mirror is a social practice which constitutes it as a particular type of object. Furthermore, manipulation of appearance via the mirror is an acquired 'body technique' (see Chapter 8). Scrutiny of the image requires the agent to take up a role in relation to the image, and the mirror can be used in different ways, such as playful 'rehearsal' of fantasy scenarios or serious inspection of a uniform.

Networks and the socially situated self

It is interesting that Mead uses the expression 'taking the role of the other' in his description of the process whereby we become aware of ourselves. The sociological concept of roles was not very developed at his time of writing and he perhaps uses the term only to indicate that others are available to the infant, initially, in the form of distinctive packages of behaviour which she can imitate and appropriate. However, the implication is that the infant is involved in social systems (comprising interdependent roles) from the moment of her birth and that she develops a sense of self within these systems. There is, in other words, a 'structural' aspect to what Mead is arguing.

This structural aspect is no less important in his account of adult life. Actors are primarily *inter*actors for Mead. We are all located in multiple networks, some formal, others informal. And much of what we do involves negotiation within these networks, both with concrete others and with network-specific emergent norms, values and so on. We are enmeshed in family networks, friendship networks, formal workplace networks, informal work-based networks, leisure networks and so on. We are linked to government through tax payments and welfare services. And we are plugged into various 'broadcast' networks, via the radio, television and internet. Each of these networks may support us in various ways, but each equally makes demands upon us. And each is a source of information. Action is interaction.

Moreover, networks and relationships involve power balances in Elias's sense (see Chapter 2). To be in a relationship with others is to be interdependent with them and interdependence generates 'levers' of control. In some cases this power balance may indeed be balanced. Two friends may depend upon one another for the same things, for example, and to the same degree, such that neither is particularly advantaged. Likewise, a relationship and thus the power it involves may be weak. I do not depend upon my corner shop owner to any great extent, for example, since there is a shop on the other corner too; and she does not depend greatly upon me as I buy only a newspaper and am one of many independent customers. Neither of us has much leverage in relation to the other, therefore. However, levels of interdependence can be high and imbalanced, generating considerable constraints. This may be a matter of external constraints, as, for example, when one individual forces another to do something that they do not wish to do or prevents them from doing what they do wish to do. It might equally be internal, however, as when an agent avoids doing something they would like to do in anticipation of the response of another. Mead builds this into his account of the development of reflexivity and a sense of self. He notes that the infant is particularly likely to appropriate the roles of those 'whom in some sense control him [sic] and on whom he depends' (Mead 1967: 160), that is, those in relations of power relative to him.

The interdependence involved here is not necessarily material. It may be emotional. If I love another person I may do as they wish because I do not wish to hurt or anger them or to lose their love. My love for them is a form of dependence upon them. On the other hand, interdependence may be material. My boss can 'pull my strings' because he pays my wages, which I need.

Amongst the social demands and stimuli that the agent is subject to within their networks will be some concerning the body. Parents, bosses and religious leaders may lay down relatively formal rules regarding appearance, for example; rules which they are in a good position to enforce. And friends might play this same role, informally, by way of peer pressure. We know what our friends will think if we change our appearance or behaviour, or at least we feel that we do, and our anticipation of their reaction may be sufficient to halt or change our plans. But at the same time others are a source of information about new practices and might offer encouragement and support for new projects, perhaps agreeing to partake – for example, 'let's both have a tattoo'. This is the context in which our reflexive embodiment emerges; a context shaped and populated by others whose views are expressed or imagined and, in some cases, reinforced by balances of power.

Body work is interdependent and networked at a further level too, moreover. We do not design and make our own clothes and jewellery or our own barbells and dumbbells, let alone perform our own cosmetic surgery. Body work involves ideas, techniques, materials, technologies, norms, ideals, fears and desires which are passing along or located within specific networks that we are plugged into. Even basic hygiene, in a Western context, presupposes that running water, gas and electricity are pumped into our homes, and that soap, shampoo, flannels and so on are available. Body work is collective action in Becker's (1982) sense. Furthermore, the meaning of body work is often shared too. Items of clothing, jewellery, muscles, tattoos and so on function as what Mead (1967) calls 'significant symbols', albeit sometimes only within subcultural contexts. They have the same meaning for those who bear them as for those who perceive them because they are commonly coded within and through acts of communication. I know what colours to wear and what accessories to use to cultivate a 'goth' image, for example, because this image is pre-categorized within culture. Likewise, I know how to look smart or causal (see also Barthes 1990).

Desire and the other

Mead's perspective is informed by that of Hegel (1979; see also Joas 1985; Honneth 1995). Following Hegel, he views the process whereby individuals and groups learn to appropriate one another's perspectives as a move from particularity towards universality; our minds and cultures are expanded by incorporating different viewpoints as we overcome the limitations imposed by our particular situation. At the same time, however, again following Hegel, Mead believes that this widening of horizons generates interdependence (and thus social relations), desire and struggle. Awareness of the perspectives of others awakens a desire for recognition. Knowing that they judge us we want them to judge us well, and knowing that we exist within their field of consciousness we want them to experience and recognize us as subjects. Awareness of the particularity of our own perspective makes us seek their validation. We need others to recognize the meaning of what we do in order for it to have meaning for us. This can generate social conformity and cohesion. Agents win approval by toeing the line. However, Hegel (1979) famously argues that this desire for recognition generates dynamics of struggle and conflict, particularly as agents often want their particularity to be recognized above that of the other. Mead utilizes this double edge in his account, viewing the desire for recognition as an impulse which can generate cohesion and conformity but also conflict and change.

Honneth (1995) has argued that desire and struggles for recognition emerge at three levels. First, there is a search for love within the family and intimate relations. Second, there are struggles of certain collectives and groups for the recognition enshrined in law and citizenship status – for example, the struggles of working-class movements, black civil rights groups and suffragettes. Finally, Honneth refers to struggles for distinction. Agents and groups are often not content to be recognized as equal to others, he notes. They want to stand out from the crowd as an individual or to form an elite.

Each of Honneth's three levels is potentially relevant to our focus and each is present in Mead's work. Honneth's third level is the most relevant, however, because there is a good prima facie case for arguing that much body work is motivated by the desire for individual recognition and distinction. Interestingly, Mead uses a body example in his key discussion of the desire for recognition. Our self must be recognized by others, he argues, 'to have the very values we want to have belong to it'. But this is not enough because 'there is a demand, a constant demand, to realise oneself in some sort of superiority over those around us' (Mead 1967: 205). He continues:

> We may come back to matters of speech and dress, to a capacity for remembering, to this, that or the other thing – but always to things in which we stand out above people. We are careful, of course, not to directly plume ourselves. It would seem childish to intimate that we take satisfaction in showing that we can do something better than others. We take a great deal of pains to cover up such a situation; but actually we are vastly gratified.
>
> (Mead 1967: 205)

Our bodily appearance is central to our striving for recognition because it is how we exist for others.

The impression that Mead gives in the above quote is of a strategic agent who actively manages the impressions others have of them in order to secure recognition. In many respects he anticipates Goffman (1959) here. This active side is important. We can and do select what others perceive of us, to some degree. However, there is another side to this. As the notion of a desire for recognition suggests, agents experience a need for recognition and are thus dependent upon one another. The agent may cleverly manage her presentations of self, but this is not gratuitous. She is responding to a felt need to be recognized in particular ways congruent with her sense of her own identity and self-esteem. Each needs the other and they are therefore, to reiterate a central theme of this book, bound up in relations of mutual interdependence.

Self-control, dialogue and autonomy

Viewing ourselves from the perspectives of others is part of a process whereby certain impulses and actions are inhibited or controlled. We stop ourselves acting in order to consider consequences and alternatives. Such self-control is a prerequisite of individual autonomy for Mead, even if it is also a mechanism of social control. It affords the agent an opportunity to reflect upon possible courses of action, to analyse her motivations and reasons for action and to choose better means for attaining her ends or even better ends. This does not always work. Impulses can be too quick, strong or unexpected. Likewise, our level of self-monitoring varies. When I play sport, for example, I cannot afford the time to stop and think. An element of control is present most of the time, however, affording us the possibility of choice. Integral to this, moreover, is the process of dialogue. Although certain norms may be regarded as inviolable and certain relations tyrannical, the agent's relations with others, and thus the relation that they form with their self, is dialogical. Views and intentions are expressed, perhaps criticized, then defended or modified, and so on. Anticipating criticism or even punitive sanctions is only a consideration in this dialogue, something to be weighed up. It is not, as Foucault's internal policing mechanism appears to be, necessarily overpowering and determinate – although it may be on some occasions and it is an empirical question as to when it is and when it is not. Agents dialogue with their others, both real and imagined. Moreover, different others can be brought to bear upon one another. An agent may feel the pressure of 'the fashion–beauty complex' internally, for example, but may alleviate that pressure by adopting a feminist perspective upon it, which they have acquired through participation in the feminist movement. Alternatively, they may feel the pressure of feminist critiques of beautification but develop their own critique of the feminist critiques, arriving at a view that beauty treatments are politically acceptable and fun, such that they are inclined to use them.

When action is not impulsive and when not completely dominated by the perspective of the other, it is rational in a 'communicative' sense (see Habermas 1991). The agent weighs up different viewpoints and plays them off against one another, adding in and evaluating their own initial views. Having said this, 'spontaneous' and pre-reflective action is not necessary 'irrational'. Pre-reflective actions are shaped by cultural schemas, internalized rules, acquired know-how and understanding, and they are flexible, innovative and adaptive. Like the sports player, the social agent can act without thinking in a way which is both consistent with social rules and yet strategically advantageous to them.

Reflexive embodiment

Mead's framework is essential to a proper grasp of reflexive embodiment. He allows us to develop the thought that, as embodied beings, we can be absent from our own experience in certain respects but present in certain others; subjects and agents on the one hand but objects on the other. He gives the names I and me to the fundamental distinction between these modalities: the I is the active, experiencing agent who is, by necessity, absent within their own stream of experience; the Me is the body as object, present to consciousness and available for manipulation through body projects and body work. In addition, Mead strikes an important balance between two opposing tendencies in the literature we examined in Part One. His agents are embedded in social networks and power relations that affect them in a variety of ways, and their reflexivity is dependent upon this; reflexivity and selfhood presuppose the agent assuming the perspective of either specific or generalized others towards themselves. However, this does not result in total domination of the self by others. Agents are dialogical and able to answer back. What happens, how they act, depends upon this dialogue.

The position that we have arrived at is not only a 'happy medium' between two unsatisfactory extremes, however. In some cases the extreme may be closer to the truth. In some instances, for example, our reflexivity may amount to self-policing. In other instances it may count for nothing as we know that the consequences of not doing what is expected of us are too great for us to contemplate non-compliance. In others still there may be little or no guidance as to how we should act. The point is that Mead does not commit us to any one view by theoretical diktat. His theory allows for a range of possibilities and encourages us to get out and have a look at which conditions hold where. It allows for the variable and differentiated territory I referred to in the Introduction to Part Two. In Chapter 9, I will attempt to map that territory. First, however, it is necessary to take a closer look at the practices of reflexive embodiment.

8 Reflexive body techniques *and* social networks

Having established a conception of embodied and reflexive agency in Chapter 7, I turn now to practices of bodily maintenance and modification, which I theorize, adapting a concept from Marcel Mauss (1979), as 'reflexive body techniques' (RBTs). The chapter builds on the previous one in three respects. First, it focuses upon what embodied agents do to 'their bodies' that is reflexive and how they do it. We move, in other words, from agents' conceptions of their own bodies to their body work. Second, the concept of RBTs, as I will show, affords further purchase upon the process by which an agent achieves a reflexive and temporal distinction between I and me and thus an embodied sense of self. Finally, I link the concept of RBTs to a conception of social networks, thereby returning to a key aspect of my concept of agency and self. Reflexive agency is generated in the context of social interactions and relations, and these same relations and interactions are the means by which RBTs move through the social body.

I begin with a brief discussion of Mauss's reflections on body techniques, followed by sections on RBTs and their relation to selfhood. Finally, I consider the diffusion of RBTs within social networks, returning to a key contention from the Introduction to Part Two, namely that different RBTs, as I now conceptualize them, have different patterns of diffusion and are embedded in different social dynamics and logics. This paves the way for the final chapter, where I will expand upon these claims and explore them empirically.

Mauss on body techniques

Mauss (1979) arrived at the concept of body techniques after observing both that certain embodied practices (e.g. spitting, hunting techniques and eating with a knife and fork) are specific to particular societies, and that others vary considerably in style across societies and social groups. Women walk differently from men, the bourgeoisie talk differently from the proletariat, the French military march and dig differently from British troops and so on. Building on these observations, he defines body techniques as 'ways in which from society to society men [*sic*] know how to use their bodies' (Mauss 1979: 97). This definition is potentially problematic as it can seem to suggest that 'men' and 'their bodies' are distinct. Given the way in which Mauss pursues his point, however, it is reasonable to assume that this is not his intention. Indeed, he makes a sophisticated innovation in non-dualistic sociology.

Mauss's description of body techniques as 'habitus', which precedes both Elias's and Bourdieu's uses (see Chapter 2), is an important point of entry for grasping this innovation. 'Habitus', he explains, is a Latin rendering of the Greek 'hexis' (or what he calls 'exis'), a concept which is central to Aristotle's (1955) philosophy, wherein it denotes acquired and embodied dispositions[1] which constitute forms of practical reason or wisdom. Body techniques have a double edge in this definition. They are forms of embodied, pre-reflective understanding or knowledge. But they are also social. They emerge and spread within a collective context, as the result of interaction, such that they belong to specific social groups:

> I have had this notion of the social nature of '*the habitus*' for many years. Please note that I use the Latin word – it should be understood in France – *habitus*. The word translates infinitely better than '*habitude*' (habit or custom), the '*exis*', the 'acquired ability' and 'faculty' of Aristotle (who was a psychologist). ... These 'habits' do not vary just with individuals and their imitations; they vary between societies, educations, proprieties and fashions, prestiges. In them we should see the techniques and work of collective and individual practical reason rather than, in the ordinary way, merely the soul and its repetitive faculties.
>
> (Mauss 1979: 101)

I return to the question of how body techniques distinguish and differentiate social groups later. Here I am interested in the manner in which the concept simultaneously holds together social, corporeal and cognitive elements (see also Lévi-Strauss 1987). Body techniques are social facts. They vary across societies and social groups. They pre-exist and will outlive the specific individuals who practise them at any point in time. Mauss even seeks to show – albeit somewhat problematically (Crossley 1995, 2004a) – that they 'constrain' agents. At the same time, however, they presuppose biological structures and embody knowledge, reason and psychological properties. Styles of walking vary across social groups, for example, indicating a social basis, but all of these different styles presuppose bipedalism, not to mention the plasticity and intelligence which allow the organism to invent or learn different ways of walking. Furthermore, styles of walking embody under-standing and knowledge. Switching to tip-toes when silence is required, for example, indicates a grasp of the conditions most conducive to minimizing noise, whilst walking a tightrope – and indeed walking per se – requires a practical grasp of principles of balance, force and so on. When we adjust our posture to steady ourselves we engage in practical physics. Finally, certain styles of walking, such as a proud march or arrogant strut, embody an attitude and may be employed as a means of 'emotion management' (Hochschild 2003). Adopting a confident posture, for example, can be a way of inducing a confident mood (Crossley 2004c).

The 'mindful' aspect of body techniques is not very well developed in Mauss's work and its lack of development is one amongst a number of problems. We need to engage more seriously with the embodied subjectivity and agency he hints at, drawing upon the work of other writers who have developed this theme, including Mead (1967), whom we discussed in Chapter 7 (see also Ryle 1949; Merleau-Ponty 1962, 1965; Crossley 2001). And we need both to recognize more flexibility and room for imagination and improvisation in bodily action than he does and to do more to grasp the link between body techniques and the contexts in which they are practised (Crossley 1995, 2004a). The sociality of body techniques, for Mauss, consists in their group specificity, but we must recognize also a form of sociality which consists in the way in which their performance is shaped to meet the interactive exigencies of specific situations (Crossley 1995, 2004a). None of this detracts from the importance of Mauss's innovation, however.

Body techniques are culturally embedded and, as such, often have symbolic and normative significance. Hunting techniques may embody ritual aspects which connect them, symbolically, with religious beliefs, for example, and they may be normatively regulated in accordance with those same beliefs. Moreover, the symbolic meaning and normativity of techniques may be contested. Exercise is valorized by some groups in our society, for example, but derided by others. Some associate it with happiness, vitality and play, whilst others deem it square and boring, if not oppressive. American high school 'jocks' and their detractors respectively illustrate this point. Such symbolic and normative frameworks and contentions are important. However, we should not lose sight of the embodied knowledge involved in body techniques. Effective hunting requires practical mastery of weapons, movements, prey and the hunting environment, for example, all of which are practical forms of 'understanding'. Likewise, throwing a baseball demands a certain practical grasp of the ways in which the body can and does move; of the movement of objects through space; of the amount of force and necessary flight path required to make a ball land in the glove of a teammate at a distance which itself is estimated (practically, in the throw itself) on the basis of prior experience. The knowledge of the baseball player is quite different from that of the physicist, being tacitly embedded in skill and not available to discursive reflection, but it covers similar ground.

Reflexive body techniques

Much of Mauss's essay is devoted to an attempt to catalogue body techniques according to their purposes and attributes. My concept of 'reflexive body techniques' extends this effort. RBTs, as I define them, are those body techniques whose primary purpose is to work back upon the body so as to modify, maintain or thematize it in some way. This might involve two embodied agents. Hairdressing, massage, dental work and cosmetic surgery, for example, usually entail that one 'body' is worked upon, physically, by others. It might even be extended to include the use of medicines, which have to be physically prepared and consumed (this is easier to grasp in relation to traditional remedies, especially those involving ritual preparations, but the principle is the same for mass-produced pharmaceuticals). Equally, however, it can entail a single 'body' acting upon itself. This might involve one part of the body being used to modify or maintain another part; for example, when I use my hand to brush my hair or clean my teeth. Or it might entail total immersion in a stream of activity. When I jog, for example, I launch my whole body into action, in an effort to increase my fitness, burn off fat, tone up and so on.

Each society has a repertoire of RBTs and a portion of our daily routine is taken up performing techniques from this repertoire. We wash, clean our teeth, brush our hair, shave and/or apply cosmetics. Other techniques from the repertoire are built into weekly or monthly routines. We exercise, have our hair cut, cut our fingernails, and so on. And beyond routines, we periodically venture one-off modifications, such as piercing, tattoos or cosmetic surgery.

It might seem peculiar to regard the more mundane of these techniques as acquired aspects of a culture. As Mauss's work shows, however, they do vary across societies. And they seem mundane and obvious only to those of us who have forgotten the work of acquisition they require. As Goffman (1972: 293) notes:

> To walk, to cross a road, to utter a complete sentence, to wear long pants, to tie one's shoes, to add a column of figures – all these routines that allow the individual unthinking, competent performance were attained through an acquisition process whose early stages were negotiated in cold sweat.

It is my contention that practices of body modification or maintenance are best understood in terms of RBTs. I have three reasons for this. First, the concept entails that the objective properties of bodies are maintained and modified by way of the agency of those same bodies. We thus avoid dualism and thematize reflexivity. Body work is reflexive work: work on the body by the body. Second, the concept encourages us to identify the 'mindful' and social aspects of embodied activity (e.g. know-how and understanding), not subordinating those aspects to the symbolic meaning bestowed by discourse and not reducing embodied activity to mere 'behaviour'. Third, the concept is sufficiently concrete to facilitate empirical analysis and sufficiently rich for that to include a variety of types of analysis. As forms of practical understanding which have to be learned RBTs facilitate ethnographic analysis and what Wacquant (2004) calls 'observant participation'. We can watch people doing and learning them and can use our own learning experiences as a lens (Crossley 2004a). Moreover, we can interview participants and use archival, content-analytic and textual methods of analysis to explore their discursive trappings. In addition, however, RBTs can be categorized, enumerated and tested for statistical association both with one another and with other variables. They admit quantitative analysis. There are one or two complications involved in the concept, and in the concept of body techniques more generally, however, which require brief discussion.

1. Body techniques admit of different levels of description. We might refer to 'swimming' as technique, for example, but we can break swimming down

into different styles (breaststroke, front crawl, etc.). And we can break styles down further. Some people swim front crawl with their head in the water, for example, whilst others, including water polo players who need to follow their game, keep their head up. There is a potential for ambiguity here. Different analysts might pitch their definition of the technique of swimming at different levels and talk past one another. I am not inclined to try to fix the concept of body techniques at one particular level, however, as the concept will be most useful when it can be applied flexibly. I would suggest rather that we remain mindful of the potential for misunderstanding and endeavour to be clear what level we are pitching in at when this is relevant. Having said this, there are examples of what we might call 'ensembles' or 'systems' of body techniques which are usefully distinguished from the individual body techniques that comprise them. Judo, for example, comprises a number of throws, strangles, chokes, holds and locks. Each of these is a separate technique and judo is best considered as (amongst other things) an ensemble or system comprising these techniques.

2. Some techniques are modifications of other techniques and are difficult to specify because they seemingly lack positive content. Dieting is an example. It is defined, to an extent, by what an agent does not do or does less of. They eat less. Action is involved. The dieter often struggles against physical impulses, appetites and habits, for example, but it may be argued that this is more a matter of an 'internal conversation', such as I discussed in Chapter 7, than the overt behaviour suggested by the concept of body techniques. Does this mean that dieting is not a body technique? Setting aside the fact that conversations are embodied, I suggest that there are two reasons to regard dieting as an RBT. First, it often involves behavioural strategies and an exercise of impulse control and self-discipline, which is an acquired power of using the body (akin to the bladder control we learn as infants). Restraint is a positive action when there is a force, such as the impulse to eat, which must be restrained, and it is therefore a body technique. Second, dieting reframes the practice of eating and bestows a new purpose and significance upon it (weight loss), thus reconfiguring the practice of eating as a different kind of technique. This brings me to my third point.

3. I have said that RBTs are body techniques whose primary *purpose* is to act back upon the body so as to modify or maintain it. At its most basic this entails that RBTs are generic body techniques which an agent annexes, in a specific context, for the explicit purpose of (perhaps amongst other things) modifying their body in a particular way – for example, in an effort to lose weight they elect to take a walk once a week or to alter their eating patterns. This introduces a problematic question. Is the person who walks into town to shop using the same technique as the person who walks to the same destination, in the same way, for purposes of exercise? If not, what is the difference? The purpose of the walk is obviously the difference and its effects a different use of the body (walking to burn calories rather than to reach the shops), but is the

technique different? As in point 1, above, I think that we have to be sensitive to context in approaching this question. There may be a difference, depending upon what our analysis is seeking to achieve. Moreover, we should be attentive to the various ways in which 'the same' technique is adapted for different purposes, thus giving rise to different techniques. In many cases reflexive purposes have generated either dedicated techniques or dedicated variations upon generic techniques. 'Jogging', for example, is a form of running adapted to serve the purpose of exercise. In contrast to a mad dash for the bus, a jog entails that I pace myself (a temporal modification), adjust my breathing and 'settle into' a comfortable and efficient posture and stride. Jogging is a style of running adapted to the purpose of keeping fit and perhaps running long distances. Moreover, as a style it is publicly recognizable and accountable. We routinely identify joggers in the street. They can repeatedly run around the same spot without arousing our suspicion or concern because we know, or think we know, what they are doing and why. We do not ask what they are running from or to because we understand a jog, culturally, as a run for its own sake.

4.   Purpose also enters into the analysis of RBTs inasmuch as the body can be modified for different reasons. One might modify one's body for reasons of health, beauty, sporting success and so on. Again this might involve significant permutations of an apparently singular technique. Body-builders, power lifters and individuals who want to 'tone up' and 'trim down' might each lift dumbbells and barbells, for example, and might even do the same basic exercises (bench press, squat, etc.). However, the way in which they do those exercises will vary. The 'toner' will tend to do a large number of repetitions with weights they can quite easily lift because this is good for toning; the power lifter will do relatively few reps with a weight which is very heavy for them because this increases strength; the bodybuilder, who is concerned to increase muscle bulk but also muscular definition and 'rips', will use a combination of the two. In each case the technique is adapted to a purpose and thus becomes a distinct technique. We need to be mindful of these differences when studying RBTs.

Body techniques and selfhood

Reflexive body techniques play a central role in the construction of a reflexive sense of self; that is, in the process whereby the agent turns back upon herself, effecting a split between the embodied 'I' and 'me' (see Chapter 7). Whenever we dress ourselves, wash ourselves, exercise and so on, we effect this split. We act towards ourselves in such a way that we become objects for ourselves. Qua active agent ('I') we act upon ourselves as a passive object ('me'). The rhythm by which we vacillate between I and me in these activities will vary according to the body technique in question. An agent on a long run might lose herself in her run for long periods, immersed in the pre-reflectiveness of the 'I' and never appearing before herself as 'me' until she finishes or her body dys-appears through pain and tiredness (see Chapter 6). An agent who is cleaning his teeth, by contrast, might be rocking constantly between the positions of the brushing 'I' and the brushed 'me'.

Learning RBTs is, in this respect, part of the process through which our specific sense of self is developed. By means of these techniques we learn to constitute ourselves for ourselves, practically. Learning to attend to ourselves is learning to posit ourselves for ourselves. It constitutes a specific experience of self. We learn to play the role of another in relationship to ourselves. Indeed, in some cases where we tend to ourselves in these ways we are precisely taking over the role of another, a parent or guardian, who once tended and cared for us in these ways. We do to ourselves what they have done for us at an earlier time and have taught us to do, applying their standards and techniques to ourselves.

Certain RBTs may be selected in accordance with agents' projects of self-development and thus presuppose an existing self-definition, of course. Specific types of 'self' presuppose particular RBTs for their 'practice' and agents select techniques in accordance with the self they desire to be. Even in these cases, however, practising the technique may heighten the I–me distinction and shape the construction of the me in particular ways. Techniques of weight training are deployed by bodybuilders in pursuit of muscular gain, for example, but at the same time these techniques orient agents towards their bodies in particular ways. Performing the technique allows agents to experience their embodiment in new ways and, in some cases at least, to take on a role which, in turn, leads them to relate differently towards their bodies. By acting like a bodybuilder they come to think, perceive and feel like a bodybuilder, a process which changes their relationship to their bodies (see Fussell 1991).

In addition, RBTs can have a ritual function, serving to symbolically mark the transition of the self from one situation to another (Crossley 2004c). As rituals, body techniques have the power to transform imaginative and affective structures of intentionality (in the phenomenological sense), thereby situating those who practise them differently. We capture this notion colloquially when we refer to the Friday-night rituals through which people prepare themselves for a night out (washing, making up, applying aftershaves and deodorants, dressing and doing their hair). Performing these techniques, in the manner of a ritual, is an important way in which agents put themselves 'in the mood' for a night out, effecting an existential (affective, imaginative, cognitive) transition from their mundane, workday mode to their 'soirée' self. Similarly, in a more dramatic vein, Sweetman's (1999) work on tattooing and piercing suggests that these rituals mark a symbolic transition for some who undergo them, allowing these agents to effect transformations of themselves. Having a tattoo may mark the end of a relationship and launch of a new independent life. It may mark a decision to take back one's body after abuse or rape (Pitts 1998, 2003). It may symbolize and 'out' a new identity.

Change, transformation and trajectory are important here but so too are conservation and repetition. Many of the above-mentioned techniques are oriented towards preserving and maintaining a particular aspect of self. Furthermore, they form part of a routine. They are repeated on a daily, weekly, monthly and/or yearly basis. Certain technical interventions, such as a tattoo or cosmetic surgery, might serve to mark a new chapter in a life narrative, but others, by virtue of their repetition, function to structure time in a more familiar and safe-because-same manner. They invest the flow of lived time with meaning by punctuating it, but this meaning centres upon continuity and sameness rather than transition. It is integral to grasp this balance of reproduction and transformation in our understanding and analysis of RBTs, and also the different temporal configuration which specific techniques can assume. RBTs have a spatio-temporality which is central to their meaning. This is reflected in the linguistic duality of 'body maintenance' and 'body modification' which I have employed throughout this book. The former denotes techniques used repetitively, for reproductive purposes, while the latter denotes techniques used to effect a specific transformation.

Techniques and networks

In Mauss's account body techniques can be identified with specific social groups. Different groups have their own 'way' of doing certain sorts of things. Mauss says very little with respect to the hows and whys of this group specificity, however. Here I want to advance a few ideas centring upon networks and diffusion dynamics. At the heart of my comments is the simple observation that agents acquire RBTs from others with whom they interact and that RBTs thus pass along chains of interaction within networks. Likewise with the norms, values, meanings and identities that attach to them. This is not to say that any RBTs can be traced back to a single inventor. Many emerge in the context of social interaction, having collective – not to mention unwitting – inventors. And most are modifications of earlier techniques, which were themselves modifications of other techniques and so on. RBTs do move through and belong to networks, however, and this is important for three reasons. First, it connects with Mead's conception of the networked agent, discussed in the previous chapter, and further develops that conception. We can posit that an agent's network connections are both a source of their conception of self and a source of their RBTs. Second, the notion of networks concretizes our conception of the social world and foregrounds social relations within that conception, allowing us to explore processes of diffusion and to avoid unhelpful reifications of a 'society', 'culture' or 'symbolic order' which does this or that to individuals. If an RBT or a norm enforcing it is widespread then we are forced to think about how that level of diffusion has been achieved, what networks and types of social relationship have been involved. Third, relatedly, we can admit of different types of relationship, different channels and thus different networks within the overall societal network, such that we can also recognize, as I noted in the Introduction to Part Two, that different RBTs will be configured differently within the social body.

The notion of networks often invokes a sense of face-to-face, interpersonal relations. I do not intend to limit my use of 'network' in this way, however. The various forms of the mass media constitute important links and also nodes within 'the network' of contemporary society in my conception of it, for example. When an idea is televised millions of people know about it instantaneously and may react to or appropriate it. How effectively RBTs pass through media channels is unclear. Many theorists of embodied knowledge and skills tend to assume that they are very difficult to learn from books or television. And some studies of innovation diffusion (not involving RBTs) urge caution in attributing too much significance to the mass media (Rogers 2003). Nevertheless, the norms, ideals, meanings and so on that invest them may be transmitted through media channels, leading agents to seek out more embodied transmission contexts.

Even where networks rely upon face-to-face interactions, moreover, these interactions may be organized by way of specific norms/roles, taking on an official character. And the transmission or use of RBTs may involve power. Children, for example, may acquire habits of washing, teeth cleaning and hair combing by way of the persistence and threats of their parents, who, in turn, fear the sanctions and surveillance of educational and welfare agencies (Nettleton 1992). Conversely, power balances may block access to some RBTs. Plastic surgeons, for example, by virtue of their monopoly on certain RBTs, are in a position to demand high prices for their services, such that the network pathways leading to surgery are inaccessible to many. Moreover, such balances of power can shift independently of the wishes or actions of specific agents. If the number of cosmetic surgeons rises relative to the size of their pool of potential clients, for example, then the former may be forced to lower the cost of their services. Properties and interactions in one part of a network are affected by properties and interactions in other parts.

Power balances are an important factor affecting the diffusion of RBTs, but they are not the only factor. Drawing upon our discussion of Mead in the previous chapter, we might also point to the significance of meaning and identity. Certain RBTs might be categorized as appropriate for some social groups only, for example, such that they will not spread beyond that group. Though tides are turning, for example, the use of make-up and shaving one's legs have traditionally been coded as 'female', such that heterosexual men have not been tempted to appropriate these techniques, no matter how close their contact with women who do. The 'infection', so to speak, does not jump the heterosexual gender boundary (with certain sports-related exceptions).[2] This is also a matter of identity. Shaving one's legs is identified as a female RBT, and men who identify as men are unlikely to want to do it.

Likewise desire, particularly the desire for recognition (see Chapter 7), is important in relation to the movement of RBTs through a network. Certain RBTs or the effects of them, such as weight loss by way of dieting, can become desirable to agents because they are desirable or imagined to be desirable to others whom those agents desire. Fashions presumably work in this way: an item of clothing or hairstyle becomes desirable to the many by virtue of being desirable to a desired few. It may even be that they become desirable to 'everybody' because they are imagined to be desirable to 'everybody else'. Such dynamics can be more local and particular, however. Certain practices or modifications may become desirable only in specific small networks or even individual relationships – in which case they are less likely to spread.

Power, desire, meaning and identity each shape the relations connecting individuals to one another and therefore mediate the movement of RBTs through a network. Properties of networks themselves are also significant, however. For example, many networks involve 'hub nodes' which are connected to a vast number of other nodes. When RBTs are appropriated within or by one of these hubs, assuming other conditions are conducive, they are likely to spread. Parliament is one example of this. Bodily norms deemed important within Parliament tend to achieve a wide diffusion because this institution is connected to a vast welfare apparatus (comprising schools, social work teams, etc.), which is, in turn, connected to a majority of the wider population. The immunization of infants against key diseases (a scientifically rooted RBT, but an RBT all the same) is one example of this. The diffusion of cooking and hygienic techniques, urged by the hygiene and philanthropic movements of the early twentieth century, is another. To take a very different example, stars such as David Beckham are connected, via the media, to millions who desire them and desire to be like them, such that they can play a central role in the diffusion of RBTs. When Beckham first had a tattoo, for example, a positive image of tattooing was broadcast to millions worldwide in a matter of hours. The desires and meanings that attach to Beckham are important in this respect. His influence is attributable to his structural position rather than his personal attributes, however. He has such an impact because he is a vast network hub with millions of fans connected to him, and to each other via him. The eyes of the world are upon him, as the saying has it, and what he does therefore has wide-reaching effects upon the world.

In addition to hubs, levels of diffusion themselves have an effect upon the diffusion process. Studies of diffusion suggest that different dynamics and motivations, appealing to different types of people, kick in at different phases of the diffusion process (Rogers 2003). To give a very simple example, conventionally inclined people are unlikely to adopt an RBT that is practised by only a small minority, unless the RBT in question is closely identified with a minority need that they have (e.g. a treatment for a rare illness); likewise the self-consciously fashionable. Only the more innovative, daring or eccentric are likely to be attracted to very rarely practised RBTs. As an RBT becomes more widely practised, however, those who orient to fashion or to convention are more likely to appropriate it, whilst the innovators distance themselves from it and move on. This dynamic, moreover, can lead both to a process of continual change and to cultural 'inflation'. As once innovative practices 'catch on' within a network those who identify as innovators or 'different' have an incentive to either raise the stakes, becoming more extreme in what they do (e.g. have more tattoos or more 'exotic' piercings), or to move on. Thus, within fashion, as both Blumer (1969) and Simmel (1971) recognize in different ways, we tend to have a constant movement, as well as a constant distinction between the cutting edge and the average punter.

The normative and political nature of practices may be related to these diffusion dynamics. Whilst there is a clear difference between statistical and moral norms, there is a link. As Durkheim (1964) observed, moral norms often derive from collective habits (i.e. habits that are statistically normal) as they become identified, over time, with the collectivity itself. The fact that 'everyone does it' becomes the reason why everyone should. The collective, or rather its representatives, demand conformity as a sign of respect (see Chapter 1). Moreover, it is difficult for political players to enforce or prohibit specific RBTs if those RBTs are widely diffused and practised. Law-makers risk failure with the loss of legitimacy that causes. As King Cnut so effectively demonstrated to his court in eleventh-century England, even powerful monarchs have to move with the tides. As noted in Chapter 4, this applies to marketing and product development, too. Consumer trends enjoy a relative autonomy from product development and the latter must orient to, if not follow, the former.

Innovation in RBTs may originate at different points in the social network. Obviously there are dedicated centres of innovation, often enjoying favourable balances of power, including medical research facilities and the institutions of the fashion world. There is no reason to believe that innovation is restricted to these domains, however, and there is even reason to believe that agents in these domains, particularly the fashion domain, draw their ideas from 'outside'. The appropriation of the 'punk' look by the fashion industry in the late 1970s and early 1980s is one example of this. In this case the styles of dressing and self-adornment devised by a rebellious subculture became mainstream because of their appropriation by the fashion industry and their movement through the commercial channels of this industry. The general point, however, is that the innovation took place outside of the mainstream industry, partly in opposition to it but also partly with marked indifference to it. Other examples of innovation from outside of the official centres of innovation include the bodybuilding subculture, the modern primitivist movement and the related cyberpunk movement (see Monaghan 2001a; Pitts 2003). This is an important point. Some of the theories we considered earlier in the book tended to suggest that reflexive embodiment is shaped by a single process or source (the civilizing process, the carceral network, consumer culture) and that it is imposed from the top down, at least in the respect that it is imposed upon individuals. I am suggesting, by contrast, that RBTs may emerge at different points in a network. This does not mean that such agencies as the carceral network or consumer culture do not exist, nor indeed that they may not either crush or appropriate innovations external to them. But it allows us to complement our appreciation of these agencies with a sense of the free spaces outside their purview.

Related to this, RBTs may move through different channels and differently constituted relations, with different meanings, identities and desires attached to them, and different balances of power, with the consequence that they achieve different levels and patterns of diffusion. This point has a bearing upon my argument in the Introduction to Part Two. Crudely put, Foucault's 'carceral network', with its specific normative emphasis and balances of power, is only one mesh within the overall societal network and, as such, we can expect its effects to be localized to specific RBTs or 'regions of practice'. Likewise for the conduits of the fashion–beauty complex or consumer culture. Moreover, in addition to these vast societal networks we can recognize other regions of practice corresponding to various social movement or subcultural networks, in which other, more marginal RBTs circulate. The concept of society as a network allows us to begin to think about reflexive embodiment as a multifaceted reality, particularly if we conceive of the connections of this network as multidimensional sites of meaning, identity, desire and power, through which different RBTs and their supporting symbolic and normative materials will or will not pass, to differing effect.

Conclusion

In this chapter I have focused upon the practices by which embodied agents work upon their bodies. I have conceptualized these practices as 'reflexive body techniques' and I have sought both to elucidate this concept and to link into the conception of embodied selfhood outlined in Chapter 7. Moreover, I have argued that RBTs enjoy differential patterns and levels of diffusion, and I have sought to explain this by reference to the various elements (power, desire, meaning and identity) of the social fabric qua network. In the next chapter I elaborate upon this more concretely and empirically, showing how and why it allows me to incorporate insights from the various theories discussed in Part One of the book within a larger map of the reflexive embodiment territory.

Notes

1. 'Disposition' is the usual English translation of 'hexis' and 'habitus'. 'Habit' would have worked but, as Camic (1986) notes, its meaning has
2. considerably changed and degraded in the twentieth century, largely under the impact of psychological/physiological behaviourism.
3. Top-level male swimmers and cyclists sometimes shave off body hair for various reasons.

9 Mapping reflexive embodiment

In the previous chapter I outlined and explored the concept of 'reflexive body techniques', suggesting that these techniques, which facilitate reflexive embodiment, diffuse through various social networks to differing degrees and in different ways. The different identities and meanings that attach to RBTs, as well as the overall structure of a network and the balances of power and desire that characterize its relational ties, I argued, each affect the pattern and reach of this diffusion process. Some RBTs, for example, are deliberately disseminated to entire societies by central hubs with a wide reach, such as governmental health agencies, whose favourable balance of power vis-à-vis ordinary citizens affords them the opportunity to impose those techniques. We would expect these RBTs to achieve a wide diffusion. Other RBTs resonate with very specific minority identities and semiotic codes; they are not connected with any central hubs which might accelerate their diffusion, relying instead upon word of mouth and low-circulation media; and the force of their transmission from one individual to another is not supported by any threat of sanction except perhaps lack of recognition within a small subculture. We would expect these RBTs to achieve a low level of diffusion and to be concentrated in very specific social circles. There are, needless to say, many other possible patterns of diffusion. The implication of this is that different clusters of RBTs need to be characterized in different ways. We cannot have one theory or model of reflexive embodiment unless, in contrast to the theories discussed in Part One, this theory recognizes that different clusters of RBTs have different conditions of diffusion, appropriation, use and so on. This claim complements my contention, in the Introduction to Part Two, that the theories discussed in Part One are partial theories that we may use in our attempt to understand reflexive embodiment but only in so far as we can pull their apparently divergent claims together into a more comprehensive and also coherent picture. I used a spatial metaphor to capture this. There are, I argued, different 'regions' within the overall 'territory' of reflexive embodiment that an adequate model of the latter must 'map'. The purpose of this chapter is to begin this mapping process. I will offer my own, more differentiated account of reflexive embodiment in contemporary, late modern societies.

What does it mean to say that I will 'map' reflexive body techniques? I adopt a threefold process. First, using survey data that is discussed in Box 9.1, I examine the basic rates of uptake for a range of RBTs from the overall societal repertoire. This allows me to distinguish between, for example, RBTs which are very widely practised and those which are practised only by a small minority. I discuss the sociological significance of these differences in uptake rate as I outline them. Suffice it to say for now, however, that I seek to allocate RBTs to 'regions' of my map, on the basis of their rates of uptake, arguing that rates of uptake provide us with a clue as to the social dynamics shaping the appropriation and use of any particular RBT. Second, I look for clusters of practices which are statistically associated with one another and/or associated with gender and class respectively, as the theories of Bartky and Bourdieu, amongst others, would lead us to expect. Again I treat these clusters as distinct 'regions' of practice which are shaped by their own 'local' conditions. Finally, I turn to qualitative and archival analysis to flesh out my account of the different regions revealed by this twofold process of differentiation. The analysis merits the label 'mapping' because, as will become apparent, I use statistical methods that allow me to display and distinguish the discrete clusters I unearth on a single scatterplot chart, or 'map'.

Box 9.1

THE SURVEY

Respondents (n = 304) were asked to indicate whether they had engaged in any of a range of RBTs within a given time-frame, which varied according to the practice: e.g. Have you washed your hair in the last 7 days? Have you had your hair cut in the last 4 weeks? In some cases further elaboration was asked for: What sort of exercise? How many hours? How many tattoos? Where on your body? These questions were based upon a consultation and piloting exercise, and also a media search, which allowed me to build a rough picture of the current societal repertoire of RBTs. A number of questions concerning consultation of body-related[1] websites, magazines and magazine/newspaper articles – all potential sources of information on RBTs – were also included. Finally, I included basic demographic questions.

Sampling for the survey was opportunistic and snowballed. I approached friends, family, colleagues and students, asking them both to fill in the questionnaire and to distribute it within their own personal networks. The resulting sample was relatively balanced with respect to gender[2] and involved representation from a variety of social class,[3] ethnic,[4] religious[5] and age[6] groups, though all respondents were over 16 years of age. I make no claim with respect to representativeness, however. The sample was convenient and sufficient for a preliminary investigation, but it is clearly far from perfect.

Rates of uptake

The frequency rates for the various RBTs included in my survey have the widest possible range (see Table 9.1). Some RBTs are practised by 100% of respondents, others by only 0.3% (i.e. one person). This is significant because it is unlikely that a single theory, at least of the kind we have examined hitherto, will account for all the RBTs across this range. Some theories are good at explaining statistically prevalent practices. Others are good at explaining statistically deviant practices. In addition, the theories we considered in Part One have more or less plausibility at different points on the continuum. It would be implausible, for example, to suggest that those practices which approximate a 100% rate of uptake reflect existential choices on behalf of those who practise them, or establish distinction for any subgroup within this population. If most people in the population practise the technique then it does not distinguish or elevate any of them in the fashion Bourdieu (1984) identifies for some lifestyle practices, and for the same reason it cannot mark out distinct identities in the manner discussed by Giddens (1991). Furthermore, the concept of choice, central to Giddens's account, cannot be made to do very much work in relation to techniques which virtually everybody 'chooses'. If everybody 'chooses' an RBT then not doing so cannot be much of an option, in which case there is no choice.

The concept of 'norms' is prima facie more applicable in relation to these specific techniques. RBTs which close to 100% of the population practise are statistically normal and this might generate moral normativity in the manner suggested by Durkheim (1964). The fact that everybody does something can generate the expectation that everybody ought to do it (i.e. a norm) because deviation breaks ranks with the collective identities that shared practices generate and causes offence. Deviation from common practices can be experienced as a snub ('our ways aren't good enough for you'), which leads to reprisal, and anticipation of reprisal generates pressure to conform. In addition, if a particular RBT is practised by close to 100% of a population when most are not we are entitled to ask why this one is. And assuming that there is no other reason for it, such as basic biological survival (e.g. most of us eat, if we can, out of biological necessity), it is reasonable to assume that there is a norm in place, supported by sanctions and policing mechanisms. We can hypothesize the existence of a pressure, permeating most sections of society, which leads to the uptake of this RBT. And we can seek to test that hypothesis through further research.

I do not mean to suggest that RBTs must approximate a 100% rate of uptake within a population in order to qualify as norms. Norms can be category – or role – specific, as is the case with gendered norms, such that only 50% of a population adhere to them, and they can be specific to subcultures within a population. A religious cult, for example, may have very strong norms regarding certain RBTs, which it polices and enforces very strongly, but which show up as having a very low rate of uptake amongst the general population because very few people belong to the cult. Subcultural norms are not identical to wider norms because group members, if not insulated from the wider population, inevitably experience the lack of force of the norm

Table 9.1 Frequency distribution of reflexive body techniques

No.	Technique	%
1	Washed hands in last 7 days	100
2	Bath/shower in last 7 days	99.7
3	Brushed teeth in last 7 days	99.3
4	Washed face in last 7 days	98.7
5	Washed hair in last 7 days	97.4
6	Used anti-perspirant/deodorant in last 7 days	94.7
7	Combed hair in last 7 days	81.3
8	Used aftershave/perfume in last 7 days	80.3
9	Worn ring in last 7 days	66.1
10	Worn necklace in last 7 days	56.9
11	Shaved armpit hair in last 4 weeks	56.3
12	Used cosmetics in last 7 days	54.9
13	Sunbathed in last 12 months	52.3
14	Shaved leg hair in last 4 weeks	52.3
15	Used any food supplement in last 6 months	48.4
16	Used a breath/mouth freshener in last 4 weeks	46.4
17	Worn one or two earrings in last 7 days	46.1
18	Flossed in the last 4 weeks	41.8
19	Worn a bracelet in the last 7 days	41.8
20	Eaten 'carefully' for weight-loss reasons in last 7 days	41.1
21	Used vitamin supplements in last 6 months	37.5
22	Had or done a manicure in last 4 weeks	36.2
23	Painted toenails in last 4 weeks	29.9
24	Done between 1 and 4 hrs exercise in last 7 days	28.3
25	Painted fingernails in last 4 weeks	27
26	Used a sunbed in last 12 months	25.3
27	Dyed or coloured hair in last 4 weeks	21.7
28	Used 'quick tan' lotion in last 12 months	21.1
29	Done between 5 and 9 hrs exercise in last 7 days	15.1
30	Ever had cosmetic dental surgery	8.6
31	Got between 1 and 3 tattoos	6.9
32	Had bellybutton pierced	6.7
33	Done 10 hrs exercise or more in last 7 days	6.6
34	Dieted for weight-loss purposes in last 7 days	5.9
35	Had nostril pierced	2.3
36	Had eyebrow pierced	2.3
37	Had cosmetic surgery	1.6
38	Got 3 or more tattoos	1
39	Had genital and/or nipple piercings	1
40	Had a septum piercing	0.3
41	Had a tongue piercing	0.3
42	Ever used steroids for bodybuilding purposes	0.3

outside the subculture in a manner which may relativize it, much as Giddens's (1991) account of reflexive modernization suggests. If the happy, healthy, well-adjusted people I work and play with do not adhere to the norms that my group does then it is difficult to resist the feeling that the norm is arbitrary or that the subculture is. I do what I do because I belong to this group but I have chosen to belong to this group or at least I could choose to leave it because I can see that there is civilized life outside of it. In addition, and more to the point, such norms cannot be accounted for or integrated into grand historical accounts of 'carceral networks' or 'civilizing processes' because of their group specificity.[7] Nevertheless, as numerous studies of the sociology of minority religions and other subcultures suggest, it would be foolish to deny that such groups generate norms and pressures which shape or constrain conduct.

Thus, norms can run right across the spectrum I have unearthed, from RBTs with a 100% rate of uptake to those with less than 1%, but the form changes as we move away from the 100% figure. Norms become category- or group-specific and less amenable to grand accounts of society-wide processes of control. More to the point, the possibility that the practice of RBTs might be explained by other factors than norms, such as individual choice or the pursuit of class distinction, increases. If only 50% of the population practise a particular RBT, assuming there is no reason to believe that the practice is a category- or group-specific norm, it is reasonable to assume that pressure to practise it is not great and that agents can choose whether or not to do so. Such choices may be made on the basis of individual identity narratives, as Giddens (1991) suggests, or on the basis of class affinities, as Bourdieu (1984) suggests (see below for a more discriminating review of these two options).

Another feature of those RBTs whose rate of uptake approximates 50% is that they are 'mainstream'. They may not be compulsory but neither are they likely to be perceived as odd or deviant. This contrasts with RBTs which have less than a 1% rate of uptake. Such RBTs are statistically deviant and may, for this reason, acquire a label of moral deviance. Their low level of diffusion within the population makes them appear 'different' and, as a consequence, more likely to attract suspicion and stigmatization. Moreover, they do not resonate with the picture suggested by either Giddens or Bourdieu. Their deviance denies them the middle-class respectability that is integral to Bourdieu's account. And though they are amenable to an interpretation in terms of existential choices and narrative identities, there are additional factors which come into play that Giddens does not account for. Assuming that an RBT or the effect it generates is stigmatized, for example, as Monaghan (2001a) and Klein (1993) have both noted for bodybuilding and Pitts (1999) has noted for heavy tattooing and piercing, we have to ask why an agent would choose to do it. Unlike Bourdieu, Giddens does not assume that agents pursue 'profit' in all their actions but one does not need to be a utilitarian to wonder why agents would incur the unnecessary costs of stigmatization in constructing their identity or, indeed, to hypothesize that social acceptability usually figures in identity decisions. Agents may want to be 'individual' and 'different' but not so different that others mock or exclude them. Moreover, at least some of the practices at this level are in contravention of legal, moral or aesthetic norms, or what Scheff (1984) calls the 'residual norms' that play a crucial role in the diagnosis of mental illness. The use of steroids for bodybuilding purposes is illegal, for example, whilst non-lethal forms of self-injury or excessive dieting (not covered in my survey but statistically rare according to official estimates) can form the basis for a diagnosis of 'deliberate self-harm' or 'anorexia nervosa', respectively. In other words, these are not legitimate choices in our society. They are outlawed. And they attract sanctions. As such they do not sit happily with Giddens's account, which claims that identities positively 'fit' the individual within society.

Of course Giddens does deal with deviant cases, such as anorexia, regarding the latter as an extreme version of the reflexivity he identifies with 'normal' identity work. He does not devote much space to such cases, however, and fails to explain why some individuals cross the threshold between mainstream and marginal practices. I suggest that crossing that threshold must involve some sort of insulation from the wider social influences that ordinarily keep agents within the mainstream. This insulation may derive from the social dislocation of a 'deviant' subculture or from the social/psychological dislocation engendered by the anomic and egoistic conditions described by Durkheim. In either case, however, it is my contention that different processes and dynamics come into play here than those in the mainstream, such that we must be wary of simply applying mainstream theories, like Giddens's.

I scarcely need add that these statistically deviant RBTs cannot be explained as conformity to the norms invoked in Foucault's account of the 'carceral network' or Elias's 'civilizing process'. If anything they are likely to be subject to attempts at correction within the context of the power networks described by these writers. It might be argued, of course, that they are forms of resistance to these norms. I assess this claim with respect to two examples below. Suffice it to say for present purposes, however, that the concept of 'resistance' may help to make sense of some clusters of deviant RBTs, but it is much less helpful in relation to others.

Zones of practice

Taking all that I have discussed so far into account, I want to take a preliminary step in my mapping exercise. Given that there is some reason to believe that different social dynamics and logics may be in play in relation to RBTs whose uptake approximates 100%, 50% or 0% respectively, I propose to divide the repertoire of RBTs that I analysed in my survey into three overlapping zones: a core zone of RBTs which almost everybody practises; an intermediate zone comprising RBTs which a small majority or large minority practise; and a marginal zone of statistically deviant RBTs (Figure 9.1). There is no obvious point at which to draw the line between these zones. That is why I have defined them as overlapping (see Figure 9.1). In addition, I recognize that the position which any RBT occupies, defined by its rate of uptake, will be historically variable. All RBTs begin life in the marginal zone and must spread through social networks (see Chapter 8) in order to become

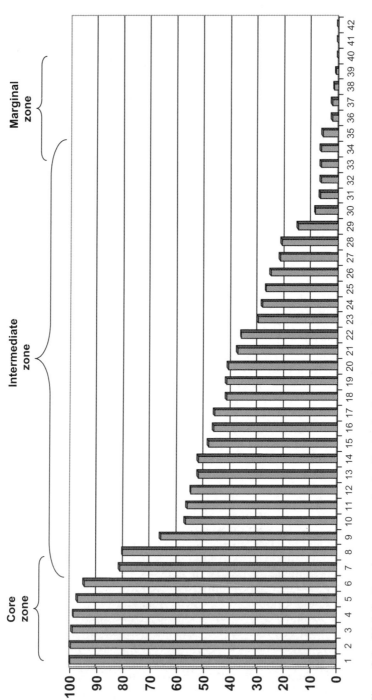

Figure 9.1 Distribution (percentages) of reflexive body techniques (bar numbers correspond to RBTs named and numbered in Table 9.1)

'intermediate' or 'core'. Likewise, once popular practices can cease to be so. Nevertheless, however blurred the boundaries or rapid the movement across them, the above discussion does give us reason to subscribe to the idea of zones. At any point in time some clusters within the societal repertoire of RBTs will be normative, supported by sanctions for non-performance and thus very widespread (core zone); others will be less widespread, either because they involve category- or group-specific norms or are subject to choice (intermediate zone); and others still will be practised by a very small number of people because, in some cases at least, they are socially outlawed in one way or another (marginal zone). My argument, to reiterate, is that we need to draw out these different regions of practice in our model of reflexive embodiment.

Clusters

I want to flesh out this idea of zones. Before I do, however, it is necessary to complicate the picture. My discussion above justifies the notion of zones but it also suggests that the territory becomes more diverse and differentiated as we move away from the core zone. There may be one social dynamic at work in the core zone, centred upon norms, policing mechanisms and sanctions, but there are several in the intermediate and marginal zones, respectively. Moreover, we might expect to encounter distinct clusters of RBTs in these 'outer' zones, relating to Giddens's (1991) narrative trajectories – clusters which have little in common except their marginal or intermediate status. We might expect to find both bodybuilding RBTs and those of the 'modern primitives' in the marginal zone, for example, but we would not expect, necessarily, to find these practices in the same place on our map because, prima facie, they have little in common except their minority status. Bodybuilders and modern primitives aspire to different values and ideals. Can we capture this on a map? Can we visualize it? We can, using a statistical technique called 'multidimensional scaling'. This is a complex technique which I do not have space to explain here (see Kruskal and Wish 1978; Canter 1985). It must suffice to say that I was able to use this technique[8] to arrange 36 of the RBTs[9] from my survey onto a scatterplot, in such a way that their relative distances from one another reflect, within a margin of error, their level of statistical association (Figure 9.2). Practices which are strongly positively associated with one another are located closely together. Those that are less or negatively associated have a greater proportionate distance between them. Consequently, clusters of RBTs, those which 'go together' in the sense that agents who do one of them are more likely to do the others, are literally clustered on the map and visible to the eye.

Furthermore, using one measure of association,[10] I found that my plot could be interpreted as a 'radex'; that is, not only did statistically associated RBTs cluster but also those with the highest rates of uptake formed a theoretical[11] centre point on the plot, with less highly practised clusters of RBTs tending to spread out from that centre in accordance with their rates of uptake. Specifically, core zone RBTs were at the centre of the plot; marginal

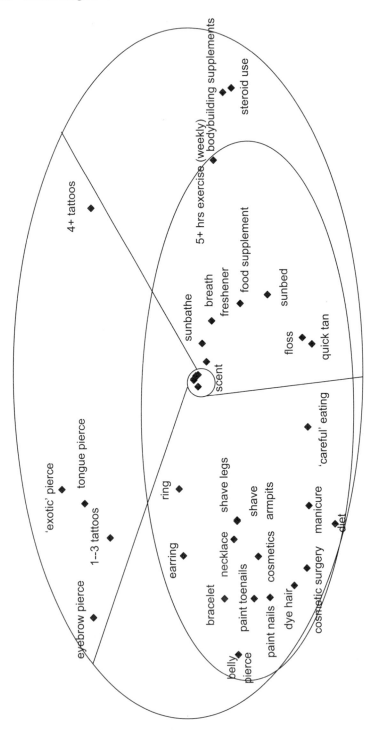

Figure 9.2   A radex model of RBT distribution

RBTs were most distant from them, at the 'margins' of the map; and intermediate zone practices fell between the two. I was able to mark this on the plot by way of concentric circles. Thus the inner circle in Figure 9.2 encircles my core zone, the next encircles my intermediate zone, and the outer circle encircles my marginal zone. The specific clusters that can be identified within these zones are demarcated on the map by way of 'cross thread' or 'pie slice' lines, from the inner to the outer circle, which segment the map.

All the diamond-shaped points on Figure 9.2 represent an RBT, and all are labelled except those in the central (core zone) circle. I left the labels off for these RBTs because the points are too close together for any labels to be readable. The practices in this central (core zone) circle are, within the last 7 days: washed hands, had a bath/shower, brushed teeth, washed face, washed hair, used anti-perspirant/deodorant, combed hair.

Fleshing out

Figure 9.2 looks like a map. Distinct regions of reflexive embodiment are demarcated by concentric circles which indicate bands of uptake rates and segments which demarcate thematic clusters. We are approaching our goal. We are moving towards a more differentiated account of reflexive embodiment. To push the analysis further, however, we need to discuss the regions demarcated on the map in more detail. I will begin with the core zone which, as noted above, is located in the central circle of the map.

Hygiene in the core zone

I noted above that the very high rate of uptake for RBTs in this zone, their statistical normalcy, whilst not necessarily indicative of moral normalcy, is suggestive of it. We can explore this further by considering the concrete techniques in this zone more carefully. The top six practices in the zone are all 'hygienic' practices, whilst the other two are aspects of personal grooming closely related to hygiene. Core zone RBTs, according to my survey, therefore, are chiefly hygiene practices.

Hygiene has a medical meaning. Being hygienic is a way of minimizing outbreaks and the spreading of disease. Any account of these core zone RBTs would have to take account of their medical rationale and perhaps origin, therefore, and we might be inclined to follow Foucault (1973, 1984) in looking for agencies of medical power/knowledge who enforce them. Nettleton's (1992) work on dentistry, for example, sheds light upon the political efforts which underlie, historically, the widespread disposition for brushing teeth. A number of sociologists, including Elias (1994) and Nettleton, however, have detected a moral element in hygiene too. The concept, they argue, overlays a more basic concern about civilized and moral selfhood (see also Mort 1987). Cleanliness expresses moral worth. To be clean is a mark of civilization and civilization, in turn, is a key value of modern societies.

This moral dimension was emphasized for me in the reactions that some of the respondents to my questionnaire gave upon being asked if they had washed their hair and cleaned their teeth in the last 7 days. Some jokingly feigned offence, as if my asking was itself a slur upon their character. Others were puzzled that I had even asked about such things; 'of course' they had done them, 'who doesn't? Yuk!' I had asked to make a point. I did not expect that any respondents, who all enjoyed access to the necessary resources, would not have performed these techniques. The response was interesting, however, because it drew out the moral significance of the techniques for them.

Here, then, we find a more substantive and qualitative basis upon which to define the RBTs in the core zone as normative. There is both a moral and a medical 'ought' behind our core zone RBTs. Moreover, it is evident that sanctions and other interventions can attach to non-performance of these RBTs. For the most part these are informal. Unhygienic or 'smelly' people tend to be avoided, talked about and laughed at. Their friends or colleagues might 'have a quiet word'. Beyond this, however, many of the services in Foucault's bio-political and carceral network police hygiene, at least in respect of those who have already come to their attention. Personal hygiene plays an important and explicit role in the judgements which mental health professionals make in regard to those in their care, for example. An unkempt appearance is likely to be read as a sign that an individual is 'not looking after himself properly' and may precipitate further intervention. The same is true in care of the elderly, disabled and children, indeed any member of society deemed vulnerable and subject to close scrutiny by welfare services.

This is a further reason why these core zone practices cannot be understood as choices. They are policed and enforced. Choosing not to do them, for many people, would have considerable negative social consequences. And there is another reason. Most core zone RBTs are deep rooted habits. We do them automatically and expect that others do likewise. They are not in question for us, at a personal level, because they are so automatic that we do not even think about or notice ourselves doing them. We do not choose to do these things because we have always done them, since childhood, and this habit passes below the level of reflective choice. Moreover, these RBTs are not in question in the public sphere either, in a way which might bring them into our personal deliberations and internal conversations. There is no controversy about washing and teeth cleaning as there is, for example, about cosmetic surgery, dieting and the use of make-up. Feminists have put cosmetics use in question, and many women are aware of this to a point where they might question their own usage. There is no equivalent in relation to hygiene, however.[12] The above-mentioned puzzlement of the respondents with regard to my questionnaire, whilst partly moral, is also partly explained by this unquestioned status of hygiene. Respondents were surprised that I asked about these RBTs because there is no issue here. It is widely assumed that hygiene is a good thing and there is no significant voice suggesting otherwise.

This point rejoins a central argument in this book. I have argued that some RBTs are subject to choice in late modern societies, as Giddens suggests, because they are subject to controversies. Competing camps argue over them, publicly, and individual agents replay these arguments, arriving at their own solutions, within their own internal conversations. What I am now suggesting is that the high rates of uptake definitive of what I have called core zone RBTs are achieved, in large part, because they are not subject to such public controversy. They are taken for granted. This is not to say that practices in the core zone will never be called into question. Nor do I deny that they may once have been so. The composition of the core zone is, as noted above, historically variable. At any point in time, however, the RBTs in this zone are generally unquestioned and this suffices to keep their levels of uptake high.

How, at a broader level, core zone RBTs have emerged and achieved their degree of diffusion is a bigger issue than I can deal with here. It must suffice to say, in relation to the core zone RBTs I have identified, that different accounts variously focus upon: the impact of early modern social movements, in both their bourgeois-philanthropic and proletarian forms (Mort 1987); processes of professional formation relating to social work, dentistry and public health (Mort 1987; Nettleton 1992); and the growth of a commercial sector focused upon personal hygiene (Gurney 2000). The content and profile of the core zone is, prima facie, overdetermined therefore.

I have stressed the 'ought' factor attaching to core zone RBTs, suggesting that they are backed by norms and enforced through sanctions. They are equally experienced as 'rights', however. It is notable, for example, that a number of influential critiques of total institutions focus upon the indignity of being denied the right to wash and clean oneself (Goffman 1961; Bettelheim 1986). Lacking control over these processes or access to the basic resources they require is identified as a transgression of basic human standards, not only by the observers in question but also by inmates. They often report finding these 'little things' very difficult to cope with. Likewise, reporting of care scandals and disasters in the mass media often focuses upon basic aspects of hygiene and sanitation. This is no doubt informed by fear of disease and its spread. There is also often a clear appeal to issues of human dignity, however, and to a basic right to cleanliness. Selfhood and identity are implicated here but in a more basic sense than that suggested by Giddens. Critics of total institutions are identifying a fundamental sense of dignity, autonomy and self-possession which is violated when basic hygiene routines are interfered with, a sense which underlies modern forms of selfhood whatever narrative trajectory the agent pursues. To maintain my sense of 'me', whatever kind of me I am, I must have control over my basic bodily functions and the interface they effect between myself and the world. Core zone norms have a double edge, in this respect. They can be demanded as a duty or claimed as a right.

The core zone, as a region of practice, corresponds in at least some key respects to the accounts of Elias and Foucault discussed in Chapters 2 and 3, respectively. Its RBTs are normative and consequently both policed and backed by sanctions. At the same time, however, they are so deeply engrained in the habitual life of social agents that they are seldom recognized as impositions. The core zone is just one zone, however, and it is my contention that notions of the 'civilizing process' and 'discipline' become less appropriate as we move away from this zone. That said, discipline arguably retains some relevance in relation to our next region.

Doing gender in the intermediate zone

The core zone is only one zone and only one cluster on the territory I have mapped. Beyond this zone we have both intermediate and marginal zones, and within these zones, demarcated by segments, we have distinct thematic clusters. The first of these clusters I will discuss is located in the intermediate zone (the second of the three concentric circles) in the bottom left-hand segment of Figure 9.2. This cluster has a relatively high number of RBTs located in it. Thematically they tend to centre upon jewellery, cosmetics, shaving legs/armpits and manicure. As such they appear to constitute a cluster of practices associated with femininity.

In an effort to test this apparent association with femininity I returned to my data to determine both whether these RBTs are predominantly practised by women and whether any of the other practices included in my survey but not included on my map have a gendered profile. As I expected, these practices were strongly gendered, as were certain others (see Table 9.2).

The bottom left-hand segment within the intermediate zone (Figure 9.2) can reasonably be regarded as a 'feminine cluster', therefore, but how exactly are we to interpret the RBTs within it? As in the map as a whole, we must consider differential frequencies in our interpretation. Some practices, such as shaving armpits/legs and using cosmetics, have female uptake rates in excess of 80%, with very much lower male rates (see Table 9.2). These practices, in my view, are very closely bound up with the 'doing' of femininity, as discussed by Bartky (1990); see Chapter 4 above. Moreover, their rates of uptake are sufficiently high to support her claim about gendered moral norms. Women may feel pressured to shave their legs and armpits whether or not they want to.

Not all 'feminine' RBTs manifest the same rates of uptake amongst women as leg/armpit shaving and cosmetic use. These, I suggest, again making exceptions for category- or group-specific norms, might be interpreted in terms of choice and identity. Assuming core gender modifications have been taken care of, women then seemingly enjoy some latitude for doing their femininity in different ways, The gender skew of this cluster of RBTs indicates that women are generally more conscious of cultivating their appearance than men, however, and this supports the point that women are under greater pressure to look good, as do the large gender discrepancies in 'consultation practices'. Women are more inclined to read up on tips for reflexive embodiment than are men – and not only in relation to appearance. They are more preoccupied with their bodies. Again this supports Bartky's argument.

What about men? Are there any male-specific RBTs? I omitted facial shaving, which is the obvious male RBT, from my survey. This was an oversight, but apart from associations between beards and middle-class radicalism, which echo from the 1960s (Crossley 2003), there is arguably little of interest that this variable would contribute to our general discussion.

Table 9.2   Gendered reflexive body techniques

	Female (%)	Male (%)	P =
Reflexive body techniques			
Big differences (with female predominance)			
Shaved leg hair in last 4 weeks	83.2	5	0.000
Used cosmetics in last 7 days	84.8	9.2	0.000
Shaved armpit hair in last 4 weeks	85.3	11.7	0.000
Worn one or two earrings in last 7 days	71.2	7.5	0.000
Worn a necklace in last 7 days	74.9	30	0.000
Combed hair in last 7 days	95.7	59.2	0.000
Worn a ring in last 7 days	81.5	42.5	0.000
Had or done a manicure in last 4 weeks	53.6	10	0.000
Painted toenails in last 4 weeks	48.9	0.8	0.000
Painted (hand) nails in last 4 weeks	44.6	0	0.000
Worn a bracelet in last 7 days	56	20	0.000
Small but statistically significant differences (with female predominance)			
Used anti-perspirant/deodorant in last 7 days	98.4	89.2	0.000
Used aftershave/perfume in last 7 days	85.9	71.7	0.002
Dieted for weight loss over last 7 days	8.2	1.7	0.001
Body piercings other than ears	14.1	4.2	0.005
Flossed in last 4 weeks	48.9	30.8	0.002
Sunbathed in last 12 months	58.2	43.3	0.001
Dyed or coloured hair in last 4 weeks	32.1	5.8	0.000
Used 'quick tan' lotion in last 12 months	29.3	8.3	0.000
Male predominance (small but statistically significant differences)			
Used bodybuilding supplements in last 6 months	0	3.3	0.013
Has 3 or more tattoos	0	2.5	0.031
Consultation practices			
Read magazine/newspaper article on beauty tips	57.1	3.4	0.000
Read magazine/newspaper article on health tips	50	10.8	0.000
Read magazine/newspaper article on skin care tips	48.4	2.6	0.000
Read magazine/newspaper article on exercise tips	36.1	16	0.000
Read any of the above	69.6	24.2	0.000
Read a health-dedicated magazine	21.7	5.8	0.034
Consulted a beauty-dedicated website	3.8	0	0.032

Men choose whether to shave or not, in accordance with an image or identity ideal, and women do not have to make that choice because their facial hair tends to be much less extensive and more slow growing. The only two RBTs with a statistically significant male preponderance that I identified were 'use of bodybuilding supplements within the last 6 months' and 'having three or more tattoos'. This is interesting because tattoos and especially muscles arguably have a 'masculine' connotation. However, as the very low rates of uptake for these RBTs amongst men indicates, they are hardly normative. The vast majority of men get by without them and assumedly experience no pressure to use them. We could approach our female RBTs from a male angle, of course. The very low uptake of toenail and fingernail painting amongst men might indicate a normative prohibition on this practice for men, for example. My suspicion, however, is that the social pressure is upon women to do these things rather than upon men to abstain. This is not to deny that masculinity is 'done'. Work by Connell (1987), amongst others, offers good reason to believe that it is. However, with the possible exception of 'muscle' and 'looking tough', it is much less centred upon the cultivation of a particular 'look'. Men must appear as men but, to echo Young (2005), not by turning their body into an object of visual consumption. Although the ground is moving, men are not for looking at and are discouraged from acting as if they were – this is one reason for the stigmatization and suspicion that surrounds bodybuilding (Klein 1993). As with femininity, this is changing but it is not yet erased from the masculine habitus.

My survey reveals a clear 'region' within the overall territory of reflexive embodiment, therefore, where the feminist critiques of Bartky and Bordo appear to have a purchase. I can lend some empirical support to their arguments. At the same time, however, as with the other arguments reviewed in this book, my map suggests that these theories apply only in this region. Some RBTs are gendered and some of these appear normative but others are not and/or do not.

Whither class?

Is it possible to locate class on our map as we have gender? The work of Bourdieu, as well as certain of Giddens's critics, would suggest that class is a key structuring factor in relation to reflexive embodiment (Williams and Bendelow 1998; May and Cooper 2001). My own survey did not unearth any significant class patterns. In an effort to better test the idea, however, I considered the evidence of the 2003 Health Survey for England (Sproston and Primatesta 2004). This survey is much bigger than mine (n = 18,553)[13] and though it does not deal with most of the RBTs included in my survey it does include a number of practices associated with working out and healthy eating. Both Bourdieu and Giddens's critics predict that such practices will be higher amongst those in more common social positions, measured in terms of economic or cultural capital. And prior analysis of earlier national surveys has tended to support this prediction (Blaxter 1990; Savage et al. 1992; Tomlinson 2003), a fact some have interpreted as evidence in favour of Bourdieu's model

(Savage *et al.* 1992; Tomlinson 2003). The most recent of the surveys consulted in this work is from 1993 (in Tomlinson 2003), however, and given that we are dealing with recent changes it seems reasonable to consult a more recent source.

I do not have the space to conduct a detailed analysis. I cannot tease out differences between class fractions, as Savage *et al.* (1992) do, nor can I distinguish between the effects of economic and cultural capital, as Bourdieu (1984) does. I can discuss some important trends, however. Consider Figure 9.3. These graphs suggest that individuals in higher social classes are more likely to 'work out',[14] more likely to use vitamin and mineral supplements, less likely to add salt to their food (the focus of a number of health campaigns in recent years) and less likely to smoke. In these respects their lifestyle is healthier than that of individuals in lower social classes. Moreover, women tend to have healthier lifestyles than men in the same class as them. The differences are not enormous but they are quite big in some cases, and they tend to be linear – lifestyles are progressively healthier as we move up the class scale. There is evidence here, therefore, to support those who champion Bourdieu and/or criticize Giddens by reference to class differences in body modification and maintenance. It is important to add, however, that this cannot be interpreted simply in terms of financial resources. Not smoking and reducing salt from one's diet do not cost money, nor need exercise, at least not necessarily (class patterns for home or outdoor-based exercise, which are either free or relatively cheap, are the same as for those, such as gyms, involving regular payment). The gender differences reinforce this point. If women tend to have a healthier lifestyle than men in the same financial position as them then there must be something more than finances involved.

In order to push this further, still using the Health Survey and employing a statistical technique called multiple correspondence analysis,[15] I devised a 'healthy eating' scale which reflects: level of fat in diet; amount of fried food eaten; amount of cakes eaten; amount of chocolate and crisps eaten; and amount of fruit and vegetables eaten. The mean for different gender/class groups is given on the vertical axis of Figure 9.4, with mean number of workout sessions per month being given on the horizontal axis. Notice first the female scores. They manifest a clear linear class relationship. As we move from class VI through to class I women do more exercise on average and eat more healthily. Notice also, however, that the female 'line' is higher than the male scores, indicating that women generally eat more healthily than men.

The male scores do not have the same linearity in relation to class. Men in social class II have marginally more healthy lifestyles than men in social class I, for example. Nevertheless there is a clear class pattern here too. Men form two clusters, with those in social classes I, II and III generally doing more exercise and eating more healthily than those in social classes IV, V and VI.

Are we to conclude, then, that Bourdieu and the critics of Giddens are right and that reflexive embodiment, at least in so far as it concerns the promotion of health, is shaped by class? There is a complication: alcohol consumption (see also Burrows and Nettleton 1995). As Figure 9.5 shows, higher social classes are more likely to drink 'heavily' and even 'very heavily'. In this

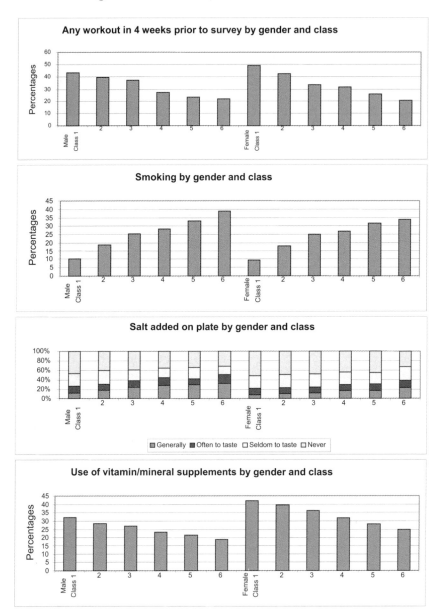

respect they are less healthy than members of other classes. This might
Figure 9.3 Class, gender and reflexive body techniques (Sproston and
Primatesta 2004)

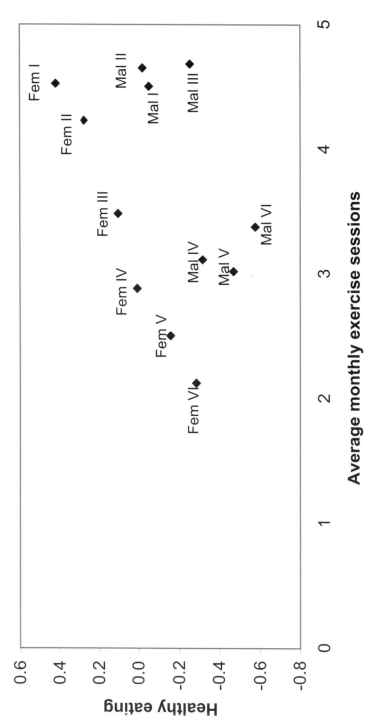

Figure 9.4 Class, gender and the space of health practices

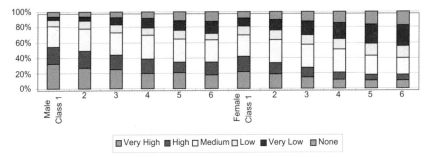

Figure 9.5 Alcohol consumption by gender and class

reflect the fact that drink, certainly amongst the adult population, has not been subject to the same level of health campaigning as, for example, smoking and salt consumption. Perhaps the middle class are more attuned to the messages of the 'risk society' (Chapter 1) and have not cut down on drink because they have not been warned against it? That does not explain why they drink more than other classes, however, nor does it attribute them with very much agency. If they are concerned about their health then surely they can either work out or find out that heavy drinking is bad for you? Maybe they drink more because they can afford to? But of all groups they can best afford to smoke and they do not. This anomaly is significant enough, in my view, to cast doubt upon the claim that the middle class are characterized by a greater commitment to the active pursuit of health.

Savage *et al.* (1992) discerned a similar pattern in their work, which they put down to class fractions. Some groups within the middle class, defined by specific occupations, are inclined to 'puritanism', they argue. This group look after themselves. Others, again defined by occupation, are 'postmoderns'. They work out but they also drink, eclectically mixing asceticism and health consciousness with hedonism. Others are a bit nondescript and do none of the above. I do not have the space to retest this claim here, but as a final point on class consider the Venn diagram in Figure 9.6. This diagram presents relations between drinking, smoking and working out in men (over age 16) in social class I. We can identify an ascetic or 'puritan' group here: 16.7% work out but do not either smoke or drink heavily. We can also identify a 'none of the above' group: 23.7% neither work out, smoke, nor drink heavily. And we have some 'postmoderns': 23.9% work out and drink heavily, and a further 1.6% add smoking to their eclectic mix. Over 25% drink heavily without working out, however, and 3.8% both drink and smoke without working out. There is a sizeable 'non-exercising boozers' camp amongst social class I men too, therefore, and the idea that class predicts health behaviour or furnishes an underlying ethos which, in turn, shapes behaviour starts to look shaky. There is a great deal of variation within classes, which perhaps points to a greater scope for individual choice and identity than Bourdieu suggests. This observation resonates with my earlier observation that the relevant qualitative evidence suggests that agents do not theorize their reflexive body projects in terms of class or distinction or coded equivalents of either of these. They tend to theorize their practice in terms of individuality and identity.

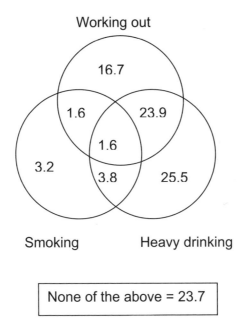

Working out

16.7

1.6   23.9

1.6

3.2

3.8   25.5

Smoking   Heavy drinking

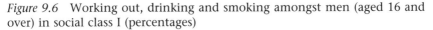

None of the above = 23.7

Figure 9.6   Working out, drinking and smoking amongst men (aged 16 and over) in social class I (percentages)

I do not propose to solve the class issue here. I do not have the space necessary. It must suffice to say that class is significant in relation to some RBTs, such that Giddens's critics are vindicated, but that it is not as significant as Bourdieu suggests, or at least is not significant in the way he suggests, such that there is room for critique of his position too.

Tweaking in the intermediate zone

Returning to Figure 9.2, consider those RBTs on the right-hand side of the intermediate zone: tanning techniques, flossing, the use of breath freshener and scent, and the use of general food supplements. I do not have a great deal to say about these practices. They are RBTs which, to all intents and purposes, individuals can choose either to use or to ignore, perhaps in accordance with a sense of either identity or risk. Some people like to appear tanned, for example, as it conveys a sense of who and what they think they are. Others avoid excess sun and sunbeds because of the risks of skin cancer, or because they think that a tan is 'common'. And the former might choose to use supplements either to improve their health, instrumentally, or because they like to think of themselves as 'healthy'. The analysis above suggests that both class and gender may shape such choices, but we cannot link these RBTs to gender in the way that we could the feminine practices referred to above. The differences are not nearly so marked.

These RBTs could all be linked to 'consumer culture'. Certainly they tend to involve the purchasing of goods. However, their relatively low rates of uptake suggest, contrary to some versions of the consumer culture thesis, that pressure to take them up is not great. Giddens's model of individual choice, based upon identity narratives, seems a more plausible scenario, and those studies which support the individualization thesis do tend to focus upon practices of this type (see Chapter 1).

It is important to add, however, that this cluster is not necessarily thematically homogenous. These practices might have ended up clustered together on the map because they are not as rare (or marginal) as some and not as feminine as others. Perhaps this description captures the intermediate zone, to some extent, but as I hope I have indicated, we might find the props of quite distinct identities and narrative trajectories even within this cluster, and further analysis would be necessary to establish whether or not this is so.

Pumping and piercing in the marginal zone

Finally, consider the two clusters in the wider circle that I have dubbed the marginal zone (see Figure 9.2). At the top we have a cluster centred upon tattooing and more unusual forms of piercing. The cluster seems quite wide, with '4+ tattoos' far over to the right, a long way from the other practices I am linking it to. This is accounted for, however, by the fact that the categories of having between one and three tattoos and having more than three tattoos are mutually exclusive and are therefore not associated. The fact that this cluster still enjoys an identifiable location on the map (in the top quarter), in spite of this methodological artefact, indicates the strength of clustering of its component RBTs. To the far right of the map, by contrast, we have '5 hours or more exercise per week', alongside use of both bodybuilding supplements and steroids. I do not believe that I captured any 'modern primitives' in my survey, and if I got one serious, competing bodybuilder I only got one. Nevertheless, these two clusters do seem to point in the direction of 'bodybuilding' and modern primitivism; having made a qualification, I will use them as a reason to briefly discuss these two subcultures.

My qualification is that further analysis of my data revealed that many more people work out for over 5 hours a week than use steroids or bodybuilding supplements – though doing the latter is a good predictor of doing the former. Bodybuilders are a small subset of those who exercise heavily. This is demonstrated by the Venn diagram in Figure 9.7. Eighty-five people in my sample exercised for more than 5 hours a week, but 78 of those did not use bodybuilding supplements or steroids and did not read bodybuilding magazines (a variable I added into my analysis for this exercise only). Strictly speaking, I should treat 'heavy exercise' and 'bodybuilding' as two (perhaps more?) distinct subcultures. I am not going to, however, for reasons of space.

Bodybuilding and primitivism are statistically deviant in our society. A tiny proportion of the total population is involved. Moreover, there is good reason to believe that, though both shade into accepted and even fashionable domains in their more moderate forms, their moral and aesthetic legitimacy is questioned in wider society and their practitioners are sometimes subject to stigmatization and derision. This point has been noted in relation to

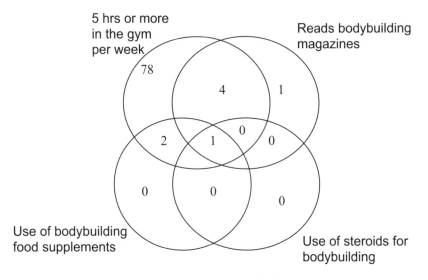

5 hrs or more
in the gym
per week

Reads bodybuilding
magazines

78

4

1

2

1

0

0

0

0

0

Use of bodybuilding
food supplements

Use of steroids for
bodybuilding

Figure 9.7   Distinguishing gym use from bodybuilding (*n = 86*)

bodybuilding by both Monaghan (2001a) and Klein (1993), and for female
bodybuilding by Aoki (1996; see also St Martin and Gavey 1996). It has been
noted in relation to piercing by Pitts (1999). These RBTs and the modifications they involve are not simply statistically deviant, then, they are morally
deviant – not in my opinion but, the studies indicate, in the opinion of many.
Their participants are, in Becker's (1963) terms, 'outsiders'.

This moral deviance prompts the question of how and why people become
involved in these subcultures. Why do something that the average person in
the street will stigmatize or laugh at and certainly not value? It might be
replied that these marginal zone practices are forms of resistance. In the case
of 'primitivist' practices this is plausible. Although the radical credentials of
primitivism have been challenged (Klesse 1999), certain of the key figures
within the primitivist world, including its founder, Fakir Musafar, claim to be
challenging the denial and repression of the body and its sensual capacities in
modern Western societies (Vale and Juno 1999; Pitts 2003). Moreover,
primitivism is associated with other self-identified rebellious subcultures,
such as punk, and overlaps with the lifestyle 'wings' of certain more radical
social movements. So-called 'lifestyle anarchists' often sport tattoos and
piercings, for example, and the 'primitivism' of the modern primitives
resonates with 'primitivist' themes in certain esoteric branches of anarchism
and environmentalism. It would not be too much of a stretch of the
imagination, therefore, to consider modern primitivism a new social movement, at least in some part and for some who engage in it. The same is not
true of bodybuilding, however. Negative social reactions to muscle are
portrayed in the ethnographic literature as something that bodybuilders are
surprised and concerned about (Klein 1993; Monaghan 2001a). Moreover,
jokes might abound about non-muscular 'pin necks' in bodybuilding circles,
generating a sense of 'us and them' (Fussell 1991), but no research that I have

encountered suggests that bodybuilders want to challenge contemporary society – except in the respect that they want their 'sport' to be recognized as a sport and accepted. Even female bodybuilders, who Bartky (1990) portrays as resisting, do not really fit the resistance mould. They do not claim to be resisting gender stereotypes and, like many female athletes, they are inclined both to emphasize their feminine traits and resist imputations of 'gender bending' (St Martin and Gavey 1996).

If bodybuilding is not resistance then what is? Two possibilities are suggested in the literature. Some, such as Klein (1993), offer psychological explanations which tend to portray bodybuilding as a form of narcissistic personality disorder, fuelled by underlying insecurities about masculinity. Others, such as Monaghan (1999, 2001a), offer a subcultural view. Somewhere between these accounts we have the widely cited autobiography of Sam Fussell (1991), who explains his entrance into bodybuilding in terms of insecurities and anxiety, and offers a witty account of the obsessions he and his fellow bodybuilders developed, but nevertheless conveys a sense of the subculture that supported his new identity and dispositions, and indeed of the social process – what Becker (1963) calls a 'career' – by which he became more involved. Even if Fussell was drawn to the gym by insecurity and anxiety, his account suggests, we can understand the bodybuilder he became only by following his step-by-step movement into the bodybuilding world and consequent internalization of its culture. His autobiography traces a process whereby he unwittingly made himself into something different from what he was at the start.

I favour this subcultural, interactionist approach, not least because it is able to offer the kind of evidence required by the claims that it makes. Klein's judgements of 'personality' are easy to make but difficult to prove, and even where personality tests are used it is difficult to dissociate cause and effect. When Klein describes the paranoia, insecurity and narcissism of the bodybuilders he studied, for example, he implies that these are qualities that the competitors bring to the competition, but throughout his account it is difficult to avoid the thought that the competition induces them in its competitors as its stakes and intensity escalate. Whichever way round it is, however, what emerges from these accounts is the sense in which bodybuilding is a separate world, removed and insulated from the influence of the mainstream. It is for this reason that bodybuilders are able to deviate as they do and are sometimes surprised at the reactions they elicit. Moreover, following Becker (1963), we might hypothesize that the fact that bodybuilders are, to a degree, stigmatized further contributes to this separation. It gives them an incentive to keep their art, and to a degree themselves, within a distinct subcultural world where they are understood and valued. If a theoretical model is to be used to make sense of bodybuilding RBTs it should perhaps be Becker's (1982) model of 'worlds' and in particular the worlds of 'outsiders' (Becker 1963).

Bodybuilding and modern primitivism are clearly quite distinct from one another and need to be understood and accounted for in different ways. They are different 'regions' on my map. At the same time, however, their shared marginality and outsider status sets them apart from the more normative and mainstream domains of the core and intermediate zones, respectively. In this respect, though different regions, they also share something which differentiates them from other clusters of RBTs I have identified. A more comprehensive survey may have picked up other marginal or distinct clusters, with their own distinct social dynamics. Notwithstanding Klein's interpretation of bodybuilding, for example, I have not explored any individual, 'psychopathological' forms of reflexive embodiment, such as anorexia nervosa or self-harming behaviours. The key point, however, is that there is a marginal zone, out beyond the mainstream, which theories of the mainstream fail to account for.

I have defined primitivism as a rebellious social movement and bodybuilding as a deviant subculture. I have also acknowledged, however, that it is unlikely that I was really tapping into these social worlds in my survey. It is more likely, with the possible exception of one bodybuilder I happened to 'capture', that I was tapping into more mainstream cultural regions which are influenced by these 'extremes': mainstream youth cultures influenced by primitivist themes and innovations, for example, and health and fitness lifestyle niches that centre upon gym work but do not extend to serious bodybuilding. If this is so then it may be truer to say of my respondents that they were pursuing legitimate but distinct narrative trajectories, in the manner suggested by Giddens (1991). They were taking a distinctive path which marked them out from others but which was still acceptable to mainstream society. One of the reasons why multidimensional scaling is useful is that it allows us to capture these distinct trajectories, in the form of clusters of statistically associated RBTs.

Conclusion

In this chapter, following through my critique of the main existing theories of reflexive embodiment, I have constructed a preliminary 'map' of reflexive embodiment which distinguishes its key 'regions'. Having argued, in Chapter 8, that reflexive embodiment is achieved by way of reflexive body techniques, I have now argued that the societal repertoire of these techniques is highly differentiated, such that some clusters of them are normative for everybody; others normative for certain categories or groups; others freely chosen on the basis of personal and identity concerns; and others still in infraction of norms such that they entail an 'outsider' status. Moreover, I have suggested that specific clusters of RBTs can and must be investigated on the basis of quite specific frameworks of meaning and identity. I have moved beyond the theories discussed in Part One, without having to reject those theories outright, because I have been able to locate their respective fields of application to clusters of regions of practices within a broader territory.

To grasp how these various regions belong to a single territory we must return to my discussion of social networks in Chapter 8. The general 'territory' that I am referring to is the immensely complex and also messy network which comprises society – a network whose relational ties are multiplex and may involve, in different combinations: money, emotion, physical force, law, mediated communication, face-to-face communication, intimacy, impersonality, role play and so on. Reflexive body techniques form at different places in this network, as a consequence of both the accidents and the designs of different groups. They acquire different meanings and identities and they pass via different channels through the social network. To speak of a region of reflexive embodiment is to identify a cluster of such RBTs which have, within this process, acquired a similar profile of meaning and identity, perhaps similar channels of transmission and certainly similar situations vis-à-vis key social balances of power. To identify one region, however, is to admit of the existence of others whose profiles, channels of transmission and balances of power are quite different.

Notes

1. For example, concerning beauty, health, tattooing, bodybuilding.
2. 39.5% of the sample were male, 60.5% were female.
3. 29.3% were students, 4.6% retired, 1.3% unemployed, 4.3% unskilled manual workers, 5.9% semi-skilled manual workers, 6.9% skilled manual workers, 14.8% clerical workers, 10.5% managerial-grade workers, 19.1% professionals, and 3.3% owned small businesses.
4. 88% of the sample identified as white, 3.7% as Indian, 3.7% as Pakistani, 1.3% as black, 1% as Chinese, 1.3% as mixed race and 1% other.
5. 30.2% identified as Protestant, 10.3% Catholic, 8.3% unspecified Christian, 5.3% Muslim, 2.7% Hindu, 0.7% Jewish, 0.7% Sikh, 0.7% 'other' religious and 41.1% 'not religious'.
6. 14.1% were aged 16–19, 25.7% were in their 20s, 27% in their 30s, 14.2% in their 40s, 15.1% 50s, 2.6% 60s, 1% 70s, 0.3% 80s.
7. Category-specific norms can because category membership and its norms are enforced by the whole group; for example, women are required to be 'feminine' both by other women and by men.
8. I used the SPSS software package.
9. Some were omitted from the analysis because multidimensional scaling is a sensitive technique which can be thrown off course relatively easily, generating results which are difficult to interpret. As with all statistical techniques and methods, one has to exercise theoretically informed discretion to get good results.
10. The phi measure of 'distance' was used throughout this analysis.
11. That is, a point which may not literally be in the middle of the plot but can be treated as a centre.
12. Environmentalists and animal rights campaigners have questioned the means by which we keep clean, pointing, for example, to problems of water conservation and cruelty in animal testing, but they do not question hygiene as an end.
13. Not every respondent answers every question and I have selected cases in some instances, but the figures remain very large in any case.

14.   A category which comprises swimming, running, gym work, aerobics and doing exercises such as press-ups and sit-ups.

15.   This is not the place to discuss multiple correspondence analysis in any detail. It must suffice to say that, like factor analysis and principal components analysis, the technique allows one to reduce a relatively high number of variables down to a relatively low number (in this case one). It differs from factor analysis and principle components analysis in that it uses categorical data. See Weller and Romney (1990), Clausen (1998), and Le Roux and Rouanet (2004).

Conclusion

Human beings are embodied. We are not spirits or minds that exist inside a body. Our bodies are all there is to us. As the expression 'our bodies' indicates, however, we are capable of objectifying our embodiment and constituting it as an object and possession: 'my body'. I *am* my body but I also *have* my body. I am somehow alienated from my embodiment, in my conscious experience, but at the same time reunited with it as I experience it as mine. The process whereby 'my body', the body that I am, becomes an object of perception, thought and feeling for me, and becomes something that I act upon by way of exercise, diet, adornment and so on, is the phenomenon of reflexive embodiment.

In Part One of this book I reviewed a number of key theories which have shaped sociologists' understandings of reflexive embodiment. Each of these theories was found wanting in important respects. The key problem that they posed, however, was that, in spite of their problems, they were each quite convincing in certain respects but also each quite different. For some theorists, including Elias, Foucault, Bordo and Bartky, reflexive embodiment is self-policing and is rooted in an internalization of external relations of power. At least some of the time it is. Sometimes, they concede, it is based in resistance, in freely chosen 'technologies of the self' or in areas of choice carved out through a process of informalization. For other theorists, such as Giddens, reflexive embodiment is a matter of identity construction and a response to detraditionalization; whilst for Featherstone it is fuelled by the rise of consumer culture; for Durkheim it is a celebration of the cult of the individual; and for Bourdieu it is the pursuit of class distinction. Moreover, Bordo, Bartky, Giddens and Durkheim each give us reason to believe that in other cases still it is linked with social and/or psychological disintegration, the key examples of this being the eating disorders, anorexia nervosa and bulimia nervosa, and deliberate self-harm.

Some of these differences are explained by differences in ethical, political, methodological, epistemological and ontological 'positions'. As such they go beyond the remit of this book. I took the view, however, that we could extract some of the empirical content of these theories, without worrying too much about their theoretical origins, in an effort to consider how their disparate claims might be reconciled. My argument was that in so far as each claimed to account for reflexive embodiment in its totality they were all wrong. But on the other hand, each was along the right lines about what I came to think of as different 'regions' within the overall 'territory' of reflexive embodiment. Reflexive embodiment, I began to think, is a differentiated social domain, and each of the theories I reviewed is describing one, but only one, of its many aspects. The argument between the theories, in that respect, was akin to that between the proverbial blind men describing an elephant. Each has hold of a different part and therefore offers a very different description. My aim, I therefore decided, was to move beyond these partial or 'regional' accounts towards a more comprehensive map of reflexive embodiment as a whole.

To make my map I first opened up the concept of reflexive embodiment by way of the concept of 'reflexive body techniques'. Focusing upon the techniques involved in reflexive embodiment allowed me to begin to break the territory down into its component elements, in order that they might then be located relative to one another on a 'map'. The map I devised permitted of two forms of differentiation. First, RBTs were found to vary in accordance with their rate of uptake amongst the population studied. This variance took the form of a continuum, but I made the case that we might expect different dynamics to be in play at each end of this continuum and at its centre, respectively. Though we might expect to find moral norms, defined as rules of conduct reinforced by a threat of sanctions, located across our continuum, I argued that those RBTs that approximate a 100% rate of uptake within a population form a special core zone of reflexive embodiment which is best explained by reference to theories which focus upon norms and upon power. Empirically these RBTs were found to be associated with hygiene, an observation which resonates with the work of both Elias and Foucault. I also noted, however, that this empirical content alerts us equally to the 'rights' aspect of the core zone. Practices of hygiene are not only imposed upon us as duties but also demanded by us as rights.

At the opposite end of the spectrum we find a marginal zone of practices whose rates of uptake are so minimal that they are statistically deviant, and which turn out, empirically, to occupy an 'outsider' position. In some cases, moreover, they involve an infraction of moral, aesthetic, legal or 'residual' norms. The RBTs in this zone cannot be explained in the same way as those in the core zone since the dynamics of their appropriation and persistence are quite different. Moreover, they are buffered by an intermediate zone of practices whose properties and social dynamics are different again.

The picture is more complicated still, however, as the marginal and intermediate zones are not necessarily homogeneous. One can find quite distinct clusters of RBTs within them – that is, clusters of statistically associated practices which it is possible to interpret as thematically associated. Empirically, for example, I found, in the intermediate zone, a cluster of practices associated with the doing of femininity, some of which appeared to be backed by gender-specific moral norms, and a less gender-specific domain of practices associated with both health and appearance which at least appeared to be freely chosen, possibly in relation to what Giddens refers to as distinct narrative trajectories. In my marginal zone I found clusters of RBTs associated with bodybuilding and modern primitivism respectively. These subcultural worlds are united, I suggested, in that both presuppose a degree of disconnection from mainstream norms, but I argued that they cannot be explained in the same way. There is qualitative evidence to support the notion that primitivism is a form of resistance to mainstream culture, but this is lacking in relation to bodybuilding, which appears to be a quite conservative subculture in many respects. The two worlds are quite different and cannot be accounted for in the same way.

The evidence regarding class was ambiguous. My own survey did not pick up class differences, so I looked to the 2003 Health Survey for England (Sproston and Primatesta 2004). Here I did find evidence of differences but they were relatively small and they were difficult to account for in terms of either basic material resources or the underlying theme of 'health'. Middle-class lifestyles were found to be generally 'healthier' and, in the case of women, the relationship of class to healthy lifestyle was found to be linear (women are also generally 'healthier' than men). This class trend was bucked, however, by the fact that the middle class are more inclined towards heavy drinking. The class picture is further complicated, moreover, by the fact that the relevant qualitative studies tend to support the individualization thesis – that is, agents tend to conceive of what they do to their bodies in terms of their individual identity rather than any class or collective identity. There is some concession to 'appropriateness for work', but apart from that agents imagine themselves to be expressing their individuality in their body work. This does not completely undermine Bourdieu's thesis, not least as he would argue that class identification operates pre-reflectively, by mediation of the habitus. This is a very difficult claim to test or prove, however, and in the absence of strong class patterns in the statistical data it is therefore very shaky. These class matters require a more fine-grained analysis than either Bourdieu suggests or I have been able to give.

In mapping reflexive embodiment it has not been my intention to suggest that either specific RBTs or specific clusters of RBTs are static. On the contrary, I believe that RBTs may move between clusters and that both they and their clusters may move between the zones I have described. Once fashionable or normative RBTs may fall out of favour, for example, whilst once marginal RBTs can 'take off'. Indeed, in some ways it is the movement of RBTs and clusters across the territory that I have provisionally mapped out, their shifting patterns of diffusion, that will help us to best understand them. In addition, I suggest that the size of zones themselves may be variable. Elias's concepts of the civilizing and informalization processes are both interesting in this respect. The former suggests that early modern life was characterized by the expansion of a core zone of practices which all people eventually subscribed to. The latter suggests that the period since the 1960s has seen a general relaxation of moral norms which has meant that the number of RBTs we are all expected to practise has diminished, with much more being left to our own discretion and choice. The core zone has, in effect, shrunk within late modernity. Again I think that more historical work, exploring these ideas, is necessary if we are to further the understanding of reflexive embodiment that I have sought to initiate.

My own contribution to the reflexive embodiment debate has not been limited to my mapping exercise, however. I have sought also to further our understanding of the nature of reflexivity, embodiment and selfhood, which are each implicated in the notion of reflexive embodiment. On one side, this has involved an attempt to show, by reference to obesity trends, that our bodies, in virtue of both social and biological processes, change in ways that we do not intend and do not always, in the first instance, notice. At least some of our reflexive work, I have suggested, should be understood as an effort to cope with, manage or reverse these changes as they come to our attention. Our bodies do not remain the same if we do not elect to attend reflexively to them. They are constantly changing as a result of both social and biological factors, and reflexivity is, to some degree, a matter of keeping up with these changes rather than proactively pursuing a bodily ideal. On the other side, I have attempted to show that our reflexive self-awareness comes about by way of an internalization of our relations with others – others, that is, in the very same networks from which we acquire RBTs. In some respects this agrees with the 'power' models of Foucault, Bartky and Elias. However, drawing from G.H. Mead (1967), I have argued that the sphere of reflexivity is inherently dialogical, such that we might anticipate the responses of authorities to our body work but also 'talk back' to those authorities, in our inner conversations', deciding for ourselves whether deviance is justified or worth the risk. Sometimes the threat of sanctions may dissuade us from certain types of body work, whatever we might desire. In a differentiated and informalized social world such as our own, however, this will only ever apply to some forms of body work, not all of them. Moreover, again using Mead, I have argued that our inner conversations draw in and play off multiple voices: we internalize the views of authorities but also those of social movements who contest their claims, and sometimes also the critics of these critics. And again we play these perspectives off against one another within our internal dialogues. A woman contemplating cosmetic surgery, for example, may feel the pressure of the fashion–beauty complex, viewing herself from the point of view of this patriarchal other, but she may also contemplate the perspectives of feminist critics and indeed post-feminist critics of feminism. In some cases the threat of sanctions will carry the day but, as just noted, this is not always the case, particularly in an increasingly informalized society.

As a final point of conclusion I would like to say that this model of the agent, situated in networks which are, to a degree, internalized but which are, even when politically imbalanced, dialogical, is necessary to the more differentiated conception of reflexive embodiment that I have attempted to map out here. Reflexive embodiment is, in every case, negotiated, both with real others and with our internalized representations of them. In some cases body work remains contentious and subject to discussion. In others the cards are stacked against us and practices are either maintained or repressed through the force of habit. In every case we are dealing with a complex and dialogical being, however, whose relation to him- or herself is mediated with multiple others in the context of networks of relations which constitute the fabric of social life.

References

Aoki, D. (1996) Sex and muscle: the female bodybuilder meets Lacan, *Body and Society*, 2(4): 59–74.

Archer, M. (2000) *Being Human*. Cambridge: Cambridge University Press.

Archer, M. (2003) *Structure, Agency and the Internal Conversation*. Cambridge: Cambridge University Press.

Aristotle (1955) *The Ethics*. Harmondsworth: Penguin.

Atkinson, M. (2004) Tattooing and civilising processes, *Canadian Review of Sociology and Anthropology*, 41(2): 125–47.

Bachelard, G. (2002) *The Formation of the Scientific Mind*. Manchester: Clinamen.

Bagguley, P. (1992) Social change, the middle classes and the emergence of new social movements, *Sociological Review*, 40(1): 26–48.

Bagguley, P. (1995) Middle class radicalism revisited, in T. Butler and M. Savage (eds) *Social Change and the Middle Classes*. London: UCL Press.

Barthes, R. (1990) *The Fashion System*. Berkeley: University of California Press.

Bartky, S.L. (1990) *Femininity and Domination: Studies in the Phenomenology of Oppression*. London: Routledge.

Baudrillard, J. (1998) *The Consumer Society*. London: Sage.

Beck, U. (1992) *The Risk Society*. London: Sage.

Becker, G. (1978) *An Economic Approach to Human Behaviour*. Chicago: University of Chicago Press.

Becker, H. (1963) *Outsiders*. New York: Free Press.

Becker, H. (1982) *Art Worlds*. Berkeley: University of California Press.

Berke, J. (1969) *Counter-Culture: The Creation of an Alternative Society*. London: Fire Books.

Bettelheim, B. (1986) *The Informed Heart*. Harmondsworth: Penguin.

Black, P. (2004) *The Beauty Industry*. London: Routledge.

Blaxter, M. (1990) *Health and Lifestyles*. London: Routledge.

Blumer, H. (1969) Fashion, *Sociological Quarterly*, 10: 275–91.

Blumer, H. (2004) *George Herbert Mead and Human Conduct*. New York: Alta Mira.

Bordo, S. (1993) *Unbearable Weight*. Berkeley: University of California Press.

Bordo, S. (2001) *The Male Body*. New York: Farrar, Straus and Giraux.

Bourdieu, P. (1977) Remarques provisoires sur la perception sociale du corps, *Actes de la Recherche en Sciences Sociales*, 14: 51–4.
Bourdieu, P. (1978) Sport and social class, *Social Science Information*, 17: 819–40.
Bourdieu, P. (1979) *Outline of a Theory of Practice*. Cambridge: Cambridge University Press.
Bourdieu, P. (1984) *Distinction*. London: Routledge & Kegan Paul.
Bourdieu, P. (1992) *The Logic of Practice*. Cambridge: Polity.
Bread for Life Campaign (1988) *Pressure to be Perfect*. Self-published pamphlet.
Burkitt, I. (1999) *Bodies of Thought*. London: Sage.
Burrows, R. and Nettleton, S. (1995) Going against the grain: smoking and 'heavy' drinking amongst the British middle classes, *Sociology of Health and Illness*, 17(5): 668–80.
Butler, J. (1990) *Gender Trouble*. London: Routledge.
Calnan, M. and Williams, S. (1991) Style of life and salience of health, *Sociology of Health and Illness*, 13(4): 506–29.
Camic, C. (1986) The matter of habit, *American Journal of Sociology*, 91: 1039–87.
Canguilhem, G. (1998) *The Normal and the Pathological*. New York: Zone.
Canter, D. (ed.) (1985) *Facet Theory*. New York: Springer-Verlag.
Charlesworth, S. (2000) *A Phenomenology of Working Class Experience*. Cambridge: Cambridge University Press.
Clausen, S. (1998) *Applied Correspondence Analysis*. London: Sage.
Connell, R. (1987) *Gender and Power*. Cambridge: Polity.
Cooley, C.H. (1902) *Human Nature and Social Order*. New York: Charles Scribner and Sons.
Cresswell, M. (2005a) Psychiatric 'survivors' and testimonies of self-harm, *Social Science and Medicine*, 61: 1668–77.
Cresswell, M. (2005b) Self-harm 'survivors' and psychiatry in England, 1988–1996, *Social Theory and Health*, 3: 259–85.
Crossley, N. (1994) *The Politics of Subjectivity*. Aldershot: Avebury.
Crossley, N. (1995) Body techniques, agency and intercorporeality: on Goffman's *Relations in Public*, *Sociology*, 29(1): 133–49.
Crossley, N. (1996), Body-subject/body power: agency, inscription and control in Foucault and Merleau-Ponty, *Body and Society*, 2(2): 99–116.
Crossley, N. (2001) *The Social Body*. London: Sage.
Crossley, N. (2003) From reproduction to transformation: social movement fields and the radical habitus, *Theory, Culture and Society*, 20(6): 43–68.
Crossley, N. (2004a) The circuit trainer's habitus: reflexive body techniques and the sociality of the workout, *Body and Society*, 10(1): 37–69.
Crossley, N. (2004b) Fat is a sociological issue: obesity in late modern, body conscious societies, *Health and Social Theory*, 2(3): 222–53.
Crossley, N. (2004c) Ritual, body technique and (inter)subjectivity, in K. Schilbrack (ed) *Thinking Through Rituals: Philosophical Perspectives*, London: Routledge: 31–51.
Crossley, N. (2006) In the gym: motives, meanings and moral careers, *Body and Society*, 12(3).

Davis, K. (1995) *Reshaping the Female Body*. London: Routledge.

de Beauvoir, S. (1988) *The Second Sex*. London: Picador.

DeMello, M. (2000) *Bodies of Inscription*. Durham, NC: Duke University Press.

Descartes, R. (1969) *Discourse on Method* and *The Meditations*. Harmondsworth: Penguin.

Dewey, J. (1988) *Human Nature and Conduct*. Carbondale: South Illinois University Press.

Dews, P. (1984) Power and subjectivity in Foucault, *New Left Review*, 144: 72–95.

Durkheim, E. (1952) *Suicide*. London: Routledge & Kegan Paul.

Durkheim, E. (1964) *The Division of Labour*. New York: Free Press.

Durkheim, E. (1965a) *Elementary Forms of the Religious Life*. New York: Free Press.

Durkheim, E. (1965b) *The Rules of Sociological Method*. New York: Free Press.

Durkheim, E. (1974) *Sociology and Philosophy*. New York: Free Press.

Eder, K. (1993) *The New Politics of Class*. London: Sage.

Elias, N. (1978) *What is Sociology?* London: Hutchinson.

Elias, N. (1992) *Time: An Essay*. Oxford: Blackwell.

Elias, N. (1994) *The Civilizing Process*. Oxford: Blackwell.

Elias, N. (1996) *The Germans*. Cambridge: Polity.

Elias, N. (2001) *The Society of Individuals*. London: Continuum International.

Elias, N. and Dunning, E. (1986) *The Quest for Excitement*. Oxford: Blackwell.

Entwistle, J. (2000) *The Fashioned Body*. Cambridge: Polity.

Eyerman, R, and Jamison, A. (1991) *Social Movements*. Cambridge: Polity.

Falk, P. (1994) *The Consuming Body*. London: Sage.

Fanon, F. (1986) *Black Skins, White Masks*. London: Pluto.

Featherstone, M. (1982) The body in consumer culture, *Theory, Culture and Society*, 1(2): 18–33.

Featherstone, M. (ed.) (2000) *Body Modification*. London: Sage.

Fombonne, E. (1995) Anorexia nervosa: no evidence of an increase, *British Journal of Psychiatry*, 166: 462–71.

Foucault, M. (1965) *Madness and Civilisation*. London: Tavistock.

Foucault, M. (1972) *The Archaeology of Knowledge*. London: Tavistock.

Foucault, M. (1973) *Birth of the Clinic*. London: Tavistock.

Foucault, M. (1979) *Discipline and Punish*. Harmondsworth: Penguin.

Foucault, M. (1980) *Power/Knowledge*. Brighton: Harvester.

Foucault, M. (1981) Questions of method, *I&C*, 8: 3–14.

Foucault, M. (1982) The subject and power, in H. Dreyfus and P. Rabinow, *Michel Foucault: Beyond Structuralism and Hermeneutics*. Brighton: Harvester: 208–26..

Foucault, M. (1984) *The History of Sexuality, Vol. I*. Harmondsworth: Penguin.

Foucault, M. (1987a) *The Use of Pleasure*. Harmondsworth: Penguin.

Foucault, M. (1987b) *Mental Illness and Psychology*. Berkeley: University of California.

Foucault, M. (1988a) *The Care of the Self*. London: Allen Lane.

Foucault, M. (1988b) Technologies of the self, in L.H. Martin, H. Gutman and P.H. Hutton (eds) *Technologies of the Self: A Seminar with Michel Foucault*. London: Tavistock.

Foucault, M. (1988c) Truth, power, self: an interview, in L.H. Martin, H. Gutman and P.H. Hutton (eds) *Technologies of the Self: A Seminar with Michel Foucault*. London: Tavistock.

Franks, D. and Gecas, F. (1992) Autonomy and conformity in Cooley's self-theory, *Symbolic Interaction*, 15(1): 49–68.

Freud, S. (1986) *Civilisation, Society and Religion*. Harmondsworth: Penguin.

Frost, L. (2001) *Young Women and the Body*. Basingstoke: Palgrave.

Fussell, S. (1991) *Muscle: Confessions of an Unlikely Bodybuilder*. New York: Poseidon.

Gadamer, H. (1989) *Truth and Method*. London: Sheed & Ward.

Gagnon, J. and Simon, W. (1973) *Sexual Conduct*. Chicago: Aldine.

Giddens, A. (1991) *Modernity and Self-Identity*. Cambridge: Polity.

Giddens, A. (1992) *The Transformation of Intimacy*. Cambridge: Polity.

Gill, R., Henwood, K. and McLean, C. (2005) Body projects and the regulation of normative masculinity, *Body and Society*, 11(1): 37–62.

Gimlin, D. (2002) *Body Work*. Berkeley: University of California Press.

Goffman, E. (1959) *The Presentation of Self in Everyday Life*. Harmondsworth: Penguin.

Goffman, E. (1961) *Asylums*. Harmondsworth: Penguin.

Goffman, E. (1972) *Relations in Public*. Harmondsworth: Penguin.

Goldstein, K. (2000) *The Organism*. New York: Zone.

Grimshaw, J. (1999) Working out with Merleau-Ponty, in J. Arthurs and J. Grimshaw (eds) *Women's Bodies*. London: Cassell: 91–116.

Gritser, G. (2003) *Fat Land*. London: Allen Lane.

Grogan, S. (1999) *Body Image*. London: Routledge.

Gurney, C. (2000) Accommodating bodies, in L. McKie and N. Watson (eds) *Organizing Bodies*. London: Macmillan: 55–80.

Habermas, J. (1987) *The Theory of Communicative Action, Vol. I*. Cambridge: Polity.

Habermas, J. (1991) *The Theory of Communicative Action, Vol. II*. Cambridge: Polity.

Hegel, G. (1979) *The Phenomenology of Spirit*. Oxford: Oxford University Press.

Hewitt, M. (1983) Bio-politics and social policy, *Theory, Culture and Society*, 2(1): 67–84.

Hirst, P. and Wooley, P. (1982) *Social Relations and Human Attributes*. London: Tavistock.

Hobbes, T. (1971) *Leviathan*. Harmondsworth: Penguin.

Hochschild, A. (2003) *The Managed Heart*. Berkeley: University of California Press.

Hoek, H. and van Hoeken, D. (2003) Review of the prevalence and incidence of eating disorders, *International Journal of Eating Disorders*, 34: 383–96.

Honneth, A. (1995) *The Struggle for Recognition*. Cambridge: Polity.

International Obesity Task Force (2005) *EU Platform Briefing Paper*, at http://www.iotf.org/media/euobesity3.pdf.

Joas, H. (1985) *G.H. Mead*. Cambridge: Polity.

Kant, I. (1948) *The Moral Law: Groundwork of a Metaphysic of Morals*. London: Routledge.

Kant, I. (1997) *Critique of Practical Reason.* Cambridge: Cambridge University Press.

Klein, A. (1993) *Little Big Men.* Albany: State University of New York Press.

Klesse, C. (1999) 'Modern primitivism': non-mainstream body modification and racialized representation, *Body and Society,* 5(2–3): 15–38.

Kruskal, J. and Wish, M. (1978) *Multidimensional Scaling.* London: Sage.

Lasch, C. (1984) *The Minimal Self.* New York: Norton.

Lasch, C. (1991) *The Culture of Narcissism.* New York: Norton.

Leder, D. (1990) *The Absent Body.* Chicago: University of Chicago Press.

Le Roux, B. and Rouanet, H. (2004) *Geometric Data Analysis.* Dordrecht: Kluwer.

Lévi-Strauss, C. (1987) *Introduction to the Work of Marcel Mauss.* London: Routledge.

Levin, D. (1989) The body politic: the embodiment of praxis in Foucault and Habermas, *Praxis International,* 9(1/2): 112–32.

Lloyd, M. (1996) Feminism, aerobics and the politics of the body, *Body and Society,* 2(2): 79–98.

Mansfield, A. and McGinn, B. (1993) Pumping irony, in S. Scott and D. Morgan (eds) *Body Matters.* London: Falmer: 49–68.

Marcel, G. (1965) *Being and Having.* London: Collins.

Marcuse, H. (1987) *Eros and Civilisation.* London: Arc.

Mauss, M. (1979) Body techniques, in *Sociology and Psychology.* London: Routledge & Kegan Paul: 95–123.

May, C. and Cooper, A. (2001) Personal identity and social change, *Acta Sociologica,* 38: 75–85.

McAdam, D. (1988) *Freedom Summer.* New York: Oxford University Press.

McAdam, D. (1995) 'Initiator' and 'spin-off' movements: diffusion processes in protest cycles, in M. Traugott (ed.) *Repertoires and Cycles of Collective Action.* Durham, NC: Duke University Press: 217–40.

McNay, L. (1992) *Foucault and Feminism.* Cambridge: Polity.

McNay, L. (1999) Gender, habitus and field, *Theory, Culture and Society,* 16(1): 95–117.

Mead, G.H. (1967) *Mind, Self and Society.* Chicago: Chicago University Press.

Melucci, A. (1986) *Nomads of the Present.* London: Radius.

Melucci, A. (1996) *The Playing Self.* Cambridge: Cambridge University Press.

Mennell, S. (1990) Decivilising processes, *International Sociology,* 5(2): 205–23.

Merleau-Ponty, M. (1962) *The Phenomenology of Perception.* London: Routledge & Kegan Paul.

Merleau-Ponty, M. (1964) *Signs.* Evanston, IL: Northwestern University Press.

Merleau-Ponty, M. (1965) *The Structure of Behaviour.* London: Methuen.

Merleau-Ponty, M. (1968a) *The Visible and the Invisible.* Evanston, IL: Northwestern University Press.

Merleau-Ponty, M. (1968b) The child's perception of others, in *The Primacy of Perception and Other Essays.* Evanston, IL: Northwestern University Press.

Mintel (2003) *Health and Fitness Clubs – May 2003,* at http://www.mintel.com.

Monaghan, L. (1999) Creating 'the perfect body': a variable project, *Body and Society* 5(2–3): 267–90.

Monaghan, L. (2001a) *Bodybuilding, Drugs and Risk.* London: Routledge.

Monaghan, L. (2001b) Looking good, feeling good, *Sociology of Health and Illness*, 23(3): 330–56.

Mort, F. (1987) *Dangerous Sexualities*. London: Routledge & Kegan Paul.

National Audit Office (2001) *Tackling Obesity in England*, at http://www.nao.gov.uk/pn/00-01/0001220.htm

Nettleton, S. (1992) *Power, Pain and Dentistry*. Buckingham: Open University Press.

NHS Centre for Reviews and Dissemination (1998) Deliberate self-harm, *Effective Health Care*, 4(6): 1–12.

Orbach, S. (1985) *Fat is a Feminist Issue*. London: Faber.

Pakulski, J. and Waters, M. (1995) *The Death of Class*. London: Sage.

Peiss, K. (1998) *Hope in a Jar*. New York: Metropolitan Books.

Piaget, J. (1961) *The Language and Thought of the Child*. London: Routledge & Kegan Paul.

Pitts, V. (1998) 'Reclaiming' the female body: embodied identity work, resistance and the grotesque, *Body and Society*, 4(3): 67–84.

Pitts, V. (1999) Body modification, self-mutilation and agency in media accounts of a subculture, *Body and Society*, 5(2–3): 291–303.

Pitts, V. (2003) *In the Flesh*. New York: Palgrave.

Porter, R. (1987) *Mind Forg'd Manacles*. Harmondsworth: Penguin.

Rogers, E. (2003) *Diffusion of Innovations*. New York, Free Press.

Rose, N. (1985) *The Psychological Complex*. London: Routledge & Kegan Paul.

Rose, N. (1989) *Governing the Soul*. London: Routledge.

Rose, N. (1999) *Powers of Freedom*. Cambridge: Cambridge University Press.

Rosenblatt, D. (1997) The anti-social skin: structure, resistance, and 'modern primitive' adornment in the United States, *Cultural Anthropology*, 12(3): 287–334.

Royal College of Physicians, Faculty of Public Health and Royal College of Paediatricians and Child Health (Working Party) (2004) *Storing Up Problems*. London: Royal College of Physicians.

Ryle, G. (1949) *The Concept of Mind*. Harmondsworth: Penguin.

St Martin, L. and Gavey, N. (1996) Women's bodybuilding: feminist resistance and/or femininity's recuperation, *Body and Society*, 2(4): 45–57.

Sanders, C. (1988) Marks of mischief, *Journal of Contemporary Ethnography*, 16(4): 395–42.

Sartre, J.-P. (1969) *Being and Nothingness*. London: Methuen.

Sassatelli, R. (1999a) Interaction order and beyond: a field analysis of body culture within fitness gyms, *Body and Society*, 5(2–3): 227–48.

Sassatelli, R. (1999b) Fitness gyms and the local organization of experience, *Sociological Research Online*, 4(3), at http://www.socresonline.org.uk/4/3/sassatelli.html.

Savage, M., Barlow, J., Dickens, P. and Fielding, T. (1992) *Property, Bureaucracy and Culture*. London: Routledge.

Sawicki, J. (1991) *Disciplining Foucault*. London: Routledge.

Scheff, T. (1984) *Being Mentally Ill*. New York: Aldine de Gruyter.

Schlosser, E. (2002) *Fast Food Nation*. Harmondsworth: Penguin.

Scott, L. (2005) *Fresh Lipstick*. Basingstoke: Palgrave.

Sennett, R. (1976) *The Fall of Public Man*. Cambridge: Cambridge University Press.

Shell, E. (2003) *Fat Wars*. London: Atlantic.

Shilling, C. (1991) Educating the body, *Sociology*, 25: 653–72.

Shilling, C. (1992) Schooling and the production of physical capital, *Discourse*, 13(1): 1–19.

Simmel, G. (1971) *On Individuality and Social Forms*. Chicago: Chicago University Press.

Skeggs, B. (1997) *Formations of Class and Gender*. London: Sage.

Smith, G. (2001) Techniques of neutralisation, techniques of body management and the public harassment of runners, in S. Cunningham-Burley and K. Backett-Milburn (eds) *Exploring the Body*. Basingstoke: Palgrave: 163–82.

Smith, J.M. (1986) *The Problems of Biology*. Oxford: Oxford University Press.

Sproston, K. and Primatesta, P. (2004) *Health Surveys for England 2003*. London: The Stationery Office.

Strong, M. (2000) *A Bright Red Scream*. London: Virago.

Sweetman, P. (1999) Anchoring the (postmodern) self? Body modification, fashion and identity, *Body and Society*, 5(2–3): 51–76.

Thompson, E.P. (1967) Time, work-discipline and industrial capitalism, *Past and Present*, 38: 56–61, 70–71, 90–96.

Tomlinson, M. (2003) Lifestyle and social class, *European Sociological Review*, 19(1): 97–111.

Turner, B. (1984) *Body and Society*. Oxford: Blackwell.

Turner, B. (1999) The possibility of primitiveness: towards a sociology of body marks in cool societies, *Body and Society*, 5(2–3): 39–50.

Vale, V. and Juno, A. (1999) *Modern Primitives*. New York: Re/Search Publications.

Veblen, T. (1973) *The Theory of the Leisure Class*. London: Allen & Unwin.

Wacquant, L. (1995) Pugs at work, *Body and Society*, 1(1): 65–94.

Wacquant, L. (2004) *Body and Soul*. Oxford: Oxford University Press.

Walter, L. (1990) The embodiment of ugliness and the logic of love, *Feminist Review*, 36: 103–26.

Weber, M. (1978) *The Protestant Work Ethic and the Spirit of Capitalism*. London: Allen & Unwin.

Weller, S. and Romney, A. (1990) *Metric Scaling*. London: Sage.

Wiley, N. (1994) *The Semiotic Self*. Cambridge: Polity.

Williams, S. (1995) Theorising class, health and lifestyle, *Sociology of Health and Illness*, 17(5): 577–604.

Williams, S. (1996) The vicissitudes of embodiment across the chronic illness trajectory, *Body and Society*, 2(2): 23–47.

Williams, S. and Bendelow, G. (1998) *The Lived Body*. London: Routledge.

Wolf, N. (1991) *The Beauty Myth*. New York: Vintage.

Wouters, C. (1977) Informalisation and the civilising process, in P. Gleichmann, J. Goudsblom and H. Kortel (eds) *Human Figurations*. Amsterdam: Stichting Amsterdams Sociologish Tijdschrift: 437–53.

Wouters, C. (1986) Formalisation and informalisation, *Theory, Culture and Society*, 3(2): 1–18.

Wouters, C. (1987) Developments in behavioural codes between the sexes, *Theory, Culture and Society*, 4(2-3): 405-27.

Wouters, C. (2004) *Sex and Manners*. London: Sage.

Young, I. (1998) 'Throwing like a girl': twenty years later, in D. Welton (ed.) *Body and Flesh*. Oxford: Blackwell: 286-90.

Young, I. (2005) *On Female Bodily Experience*. Oxford: Oxford University Press.

Index